Beyond Words

REGIS COLLEGE LIBRARY
100 Wellesley Street West
Toronto, Ontario
Canada M5S 2Z5

Lorraine Ste-Marie

Beyond Words

New Language for a Changing Church

NOVALIS

© 2008 Novalis Publishing Inc.

Cover design: Dominique Pelland
Cover image: © iStockphotos / Andrej Godjevac
Layout: Audrey Wells, Dominique Pelland
Interior image: "Holy Spirit" by Gisele Bauche (p.131)

Business Offices:
Novalis Publishing Inc.
10 Lower Spadina Avenue, Suite 400
Toronto, Ontario, Canada
M5V 2Z2

Novalis Publishing Inc.
4475 Frontenac Street
Montréal, Québec, Canada
H2H 2S2

Phone: 1-800-387-7164
Fax: 1-800-204-4140
E-mail: books@novalis.ca
www.novalis.ca

Library and Archives Canada Cataloguing in Publication

Ste-Marie, Lorraine
    Beyond words : new language for a changing church / Lorraine Ste-Marie.

Includes bibliographical references.
ISBN 978-2-89646-030-4

    1. Language and languages--Religious aspects--Catholic Church.
2. Change--Religious aspects--Catholic Church. 3. Pastoral
theology--Catholic Church. 4. Catholic Church--Liturgy--Theology.
I. Title.

BR115.L25S68 2008   230.01'4   C2008-905803-8

Printed in Canada.

Except where otherwise noted, the Scripture quotations contained herein are from the New Revised Standard Version of the Bible, copyrighted 1989 by the Division of Christian Education of the National Council of the Churches of Christ in the United States of America, and are used by permission. All rights reserved.

All rights reserved. No part of this publication may be reproduced, stored in a retrieval system, or transmitted in any form, or by any means, electronic, mechanical, photocopying, recording, or otherwise, without the written permission of the publisher.

We acknowledge the financial support of the Government of Canada through the Book Publishing Industry Development Program (BPIDP) for our publishing activities.

5   4   3   2   1   12   11   10   09   08

To Louise Auclair

Acknowledgements

The seed of my conviction in the relationship between language and change was planted and nurtured very early in life. Like a mustard seed, it too has grown over time and spread its branches for others to see, lodge in and pick at the little black seeds it has produced. When Jesus told the Parable of the Mustard Seed (Matthew 13:31-32) to his first group of disciples, he was intent on encouraging them, insisting that they must serve and witness to God's kingdom in their own place. This same parable has fuelled the passion and research that has led to this book. Like the mustard seed, it has small beginnings out of which possibilities for transformation have grown.

For a seed to grow and reach its potential, its particular needs must be met. It needs the right soil, the right amount of sunlight and shade, and just the right amount of water and nutrients. I am grateful to all who have so generously fulfilled those needs in the process of writing this book: My mentors and colleagues at Saint Paul University, at McMaster Divinity College and in the Archdiocese of Ottawa. The many persons who participated in group sessions. Family members and friends who supported and encouraged me. Kevin Burns, Editorial Director of Novalis, who challenged me to speak in my own voice. And Amy Heron and Anne Louise Mahoney, my editors, who helped me communicate more clearly.

Contents

Foreword, by Eugene King, O.M.I. 11
Introduction 15
1. Language and Change: Laying the Foundation 23
2. Telling the Story 33
3. Language and World View:
   Looking Through a Different Lens 49
4. God-language and God Image:
   Retrieving a God of Relationship 69
5. Language and Vision of Church:
   Moving Toward a More Inclusive Church 83
6. Language and Change:
   Working with "Immunity-to-change" 103
Conclusion 129
Appendix 1 135
Appendix 2 145
Appendix 3 157
Appendix 4 169
Bibliography 179
Resources for Prayer 187
Resources for Facilitation 189
Notes 194

Foreword

In 1960 I was twenty years old. A young president, John F. Kennedy, was taking office in Washington. His words stirred hearts with a challenge: "Ask not what your country can do for you—ask what you can do for your country." An aged pope, John XXIII, called an ecumenical council in the Catholic Church, inviting Catholics to throw open the windows of their church and encounter God's Spirit hovering over the waters of the future. They were heady times. I thought that at long last some people were getting serious about renewing the face of the earth, and I knew it would happen in my time! I was prepared to pay any cost, be open to any change—God's time and my time were coinciding.

Almost fifty years later, I wonder what happened. For soon the young president was dead, assassinated, and his country entered a punishing war in Vietnam. Violence sapped the energy for freedom, growth and change that young, emerging countries were counting on to change their destiny. Dreams of freedom were replaced by policies of national security that in turn bred more and more violence in dealing with enemies.

In the Catholic church, at the end of the Council, the password was *aggiornamento* or renewal. A makeover of the face of the church was in progress, drawing on the riches of tradition and the reserve of energies pent up by centuries of strict and cautious counter-reformation. Grand ideas dictated new paths for a pilgrim people taking new steps in a partnering world. But then, having launched into the deep, the bark of *aggiornamento* slowed, and hesitated. Becalmed, the option of returning to port seemed more and more sensible. Was the promise of change in the 1960s all an illusion?

For many it may seem so. The only illusion has been in not seeing the breadth and depth of the change that the Council's call entailed—in not suspecting the depths to be plumbed and the treasures to be recovered. Did anyone in the 1960s, Pope John XXIII and the Council members included, fathom the depths of the challenge they were formulating, even when they recognized that reform should be constant in the life of the church? They went on to initiate renewal: affecting liturgy and worship; relationships between members; the peculiarly Gospel way of exercising the service of authority or leadership; relationships with other churches, religions, and the world—the human family of neighbours be they of goodwill or deadly enemies. The change the Council spoke of would go to the very heart of Christian identity, awakening the promise of a new heaven and a new earth happening now.

Central to the project of Vatican II was a new articulation of the basic level of Christian identity, the person of the disciple: a change in how we identified ourselves, not a change in the core mystery of the Gospel. From the storehouse of biblical and Christian memory, the Council called all the baptized, by virtue of their baptism, to reclaim a marvellous identity: that we are church. (How often do we complain about a church over and against who and what we are?) That we are missionaries, evangelizers in our own right as disciples of Jesus Christ. That we are prophets, we are priests (yes, that is true; it is said when we are anointed with chrism at baptism), we are kings and pastors. That we are the salt of the earth and the light of the world. Part of the illusion is that we cannot believe our good fortune, the foolish wisdom of God; the good news is just too good to be true.

In the years after the Council, we were excited by the magnificent images and statements reclaimed from bible and tradition (*ressourcement*), but when we were invited to try them on for size, enter them, like Peter we got wet feet and began to sink. If it could happen to Peter, it could happen to me. What is weighing down our feet? Partly it is the great inertia with which all movement of change and renewal must cope; partly it is the vested interests of power, control and selfishness embedded in cultures—ecclesial and secular. Fifty years after Vatican II, it is time to get serious about *aggiornamento*. The place to start is in reclaiming Christian identity—a dynamic and daring following of Jesus Christ—an identity that will ground change in structures of community, the exercise of leadership and the service of authority.

FOREWORD

What happens in a person who takes the risk of reclaiming the identity to which the Gospel is calling every baptized person? What happens in a community that launches out into the deep to reclaim its identity as people of God? What happens when we take a chance on Jesus' words "the truth will set you free"? We are not without clues and signposts. Answers are in the stories of countless persons and Christian groups down the ages, across our land and around the world. Where two or three are gathered as disciples of Jesus Christ everything begins to change—a terrible beauty is possible. Would that these stories could all be heard.

This book is born of one such story. The author risks sharing her experience of moving from hearing and assenting to the invitation and marvellous claims of Vatican II about Christian identity, to standing up and being counted as an owner of the Council's vision and mission. The story takes us on the journey of the author as a younger adult finding a home in her husband's faith community (Roman Catholic). From helping out as a parishioner, she begins to recognize her own gifts, discern her own call, claim her own identity as faith-filled and a minister, becoming a faith companion and educator for ministry in a university setting—a leader in her own right. As in all good stories and journeys, the roadblocks she encounters are daunting, and the temptation to give up never far away.

The book is not the record of a fireside chat or storytelling session. It is an account of an examined life, of episodes of change, that accounts for progress, faltering and keeping going. On the one hand, it empowers readers to identify and name similar episodes in their own lives and in turn examine what makes for growth or stalemate. On the other hand, the book is a fruit of the author's passion as an educator, offering a method of diagnosing what is happening in us when we grow and change, or when we are frustrated by the inertia of the status quo or victimized by the prevailing principalities and powers. Readers are invited to enter the author's personal conversation, through which she makes sense of her life when she draws on the experience and thought of others.

Examined experience is the gift the author shares with us. We are not offered a work in systematic theology or human science; but art in progress. The author speaks of herself as a pastoral theologian and pastoral educator. Pastoral theology is more an art than a scientific discipline. However, the book is full of insights drawn from biblical and theological scholarship, and from the human sciences that examine the psychological, social and educational dimensions of life. Making sense of deep change in the author's life requires a reshaping of how she imagines and understands divine persons, human persons, herself, the human and ecclesial constructs of persons in groups and communities. Concepts from ancient Greek and Latin sources are retrieved that help understand the life of the Trinity in biblical and Christian experience.

New concepts from cosmology, feminist thinking, and the disciplines of adult learning illuminate the evolving and expanding macrocosm of the universe, as well as the evolving and expanding microcosm of human meaning making. What is exciting is not that we are asked to master scientific and esoteric terminology, but that we are shown how the fruits of scholarly work enhance our capacity to make sense of life, to have a life! When I enter the author's conversation in making sense of an examined life, I find myself agreeing and disagreeing, being affirmed and challenged, threatened and encouraged—questioned in my own meaning-making. Am I a partner in the change called for in authentic faith life?

The author is also an educator, and shares with us in the latter part of the book and the appendices a way of facilitating change in individuals and groups. The method brings forward in our consciousness the resistance to change that is in us by nature and culture. The stability of who we are is a healthy component of our nature. The resistance to change built up in culture can be life giving or death dealing. However, the issue is not primarily moral change, but the change in self-vision and behaviour that growth through our gifts, choices and exercise of freedom generates. The clue for the facilitator is found in the fact that integral to change (personal or social) is the way we use language. Skilled questioning lays bare the bonds of resistance.

If we share the dream of a new heaven and a new earth, of life that eye has not yet seen, or imagination pictured, then we should enter the conversation of this book.

Eugene King, O.M.I.
September 12, 2008

Introduction

> As a people of God, we believe we are led by the Spirit of God who fills the whole world. Impelled by that faith, we try to discern the true signs of God's presence and purpose in the event, the needs and the desires which we share with all of humanity today. For faith casts a new light on everything and makes known the full ideal which God has set for humanity, thus guiding us towards solutions that are fully human.[1]

This book emerges from a strong sense of call marked by a passion for relationships, particularly relationships between God and the world, among human beings, and between human beings and all creation. I am a seeker, a person who firmly believes that God calls Christians—individually and collectively—in our time and space into the fullness of our humanity. This is our mission as Christians; I invite you to join me in seeking how language can enable us to live out our mission more fully today. In this book, you will have opportunities to try on new "languages" that have the capacity to release new energies and lead us to new ways of seeing and being church today.

We live in complex times. We are confronted with that complexity every day in our personal lives, communities, families, and work environments. The media relentlessly reminds us of it. While you probably don't need another book to tell you that, Christians do need resources to enable us to fulfill our mission in this time of complexity. I believe that the main challenge the church faces today is its resistance to undergoing the change that this age of growing complexity calls for. The change I am talking about is deep structural change, not surface change—change in our ways of seeing and being church today. In this book, I look at how language can enhance our capacity for deep structural change.

Wangari Maathai, recipient of the 2004 Nobel Peace Prize, captured the call to deep structural change with the following words in her acceptance lecture: "In the course of history, there comes a time when humanity is called to shift to a new level of consciousness, to reach a higher moral ground ... that time is now."[2] Carl Jung identified this same challenge in his claim that we can go through life in one of two ways: "One is to walk through upright and the other is to be dragged through."[3] To go through life upright, we must develop our consciousness as called for by the age in which we live. Each age demands new skills and new abilities in understanding. If humans are to live freely as actively engaged participants in their own age, they must go through the required development of that age. This is true for all of humanity, both individually and collectively, and that includes the church. The Second Vatican Council proclaimed this truth in its famous maxim, "Read the signs of the times!" In this book, I look at how language can help us change the way we read the signs of the times and choose practices that are life-giving for ourselves and for our church.

The introduction to the *Pastoral Constitution on the Church in the Modern World* clearly sets out the challenge:

> In every age, the church carries the responsibility of reading the signs of the times and of interpreting them in the light of the Gospel, if it is to carry out its task [to carry on the work of Christ under the guidance of the Holy Spirit]. In language intelligible to every generation, it should be able to answer the ever recurring questions which people ask about the meaning of this present life and of the life to come, and how one is related to the other. We must be aware of and understand the aspirations, the yearnings, and the often dramatic features of the world in which we live. ... Ours is a new age of history with profound and rapid changes spreading gradually to all concerns of the earth. They are the products of people's intelligence and creative activity, but they recoil upon them, upon their judgments and desires, both individual and collective, upon their ways of thinking and acting in regard to people and things. We are entitled then to speak of a real social and cultural transformation whose repercussions are felt at the religious level also.[4]

Introduction

Ours is a new age. The experiences in this age—globalization, pluralism, ecological crises, as well as gigantic strides in information, communication, and reproductive technologies, to name just a few—demand a more profound understanding of faith. They require us to develop our Christian consciousness. In this new reality, we are becoming increasingly aware that our normative ways of making meaning are inadequate. More is being asked of us in this era, and we are not equipped to meet those demands.[5] Sharon Daloz Parks captures the breadth and urgency with which we must address this situation:

> [Our] new landscape creates a new moral moment in history. Critical choices must be made within significantly changed conditions, a greater diversity of perspectives must be taken into account, assumed values are challenged, and there is a deepened hunger for leadership that can exercise a moral imagination and *moral courage* on behalf of common good.[6]

All of us, including the church, need to expand our capacity for understanding this new reality. If the church refuses to embrace the development of consciousness required for our time, then it will be dragged through this era. If the church chooses instead to walk upright, then we must equip ourselves for living the challenges of this time. If we are to come together as vital and committed faith communities, we must ask questions about our deep purpose and mission as we seek new ways of seeing, thinking, and knowing. We must clarify and appropriate for ourselves the real contribution that Christianity makes to the world today.

Being equipped to live today's challenges involves an ongoing conversion to more complex ways of thinking, feeling, and relating. This book is a Christian response to the call made to all humans—both individually and collectively—to walk upright. It proposes a process for making the deep structural change required for our times. Faithful to the Second Vatican Council's call to reflect upon and change our ways of thinking and acting, this book invites readers into a change process that embraces alternative ways of seeing and living as church today. This book is forthright in its agenda for change, particularly in the way it addresses change in the church's ministerial and ecclesial structures. It is about moving toward a more inclusive church in which we *all* engage in the development required for our time, incorporating and transforming our tradition into innovative ways of living our mission in and for the world.

This book is practical. It is based on the claim that no theological inquiry is ever neutral. I am a practical theologian. Practical theology recognizes that all theological inquiry is hermeneutical, involving interpretation: I name and reflect on the personal, institutional, and cultural dimensions of contemporary ecclesial praxis.[7] Praxis is practice that is intentionally reflective. In attending to our practice, we attend to intentionally reflective practice, to both the meaning and the values embedded in what we do. (I explore this concept in more detail in Chapter 3.) As I have reflected on my own practice in the telling of my story, both personal and ministerial, I have become even more conscious of particular questions and concerns that I now take to historical and systematic theology. All theologians' biases shape their theological inquiry. We all bring fore-meanings, assumptions and preconceived ideas to any text. Unless we are aware of them, we unconsciously prevent a text from asserting its truth against these assumptions.[8] In revealing my own bias, I show how my own prejudices and fore-meanings affect my choice of normative texts and the conclusions I draw from them. It is my hope that the way I have chosen to share my story will inspire you to examine how your history has shaped your preconceptions of what is real and true for you.

The first stirrings of this book came from my Doctor of Ministry research, in which I explored my conviction that language can enable change.[9] At the time of that research, I was director of the Centre for Ministry Formation at Saint Paul University, which is a Roman Catholic university that has been entrusted for more than 150 years to the care of the Congregation of the Missionary Oblates of Mary Immaculate. As you will read in Chapter 2, the Centre for Ministry Formation grew out of and in many ways transformed the university's formation of men preparing for ordained ministry in the Roman Catholic Church, which began in the late 1930s when the university opened a seminary.

Working closely with the centre's formation team, I was eager to find ways to incorporate the centre's vision of moving toward a more inclusive church into its ministry formation process. Although we were committed to the significant changes required by the centre's vision of ministry and church, we experienced futility in our attempts to consciously integrate those changes into candidates' overall formation. We were concerned that the centre's vision had very little impact on the candidates' practice of ministry and church. This book builds on my preliminary research on the "immunity-to-change language technology" pioneered by Robert Kegan and Lisa Laskow Lahey in their book *How the Way We Talk Can Change the Way We Work: Seven Languages for Transformation*.[10] I will share the fruit of my ongoing research in Chapter 6.

Since completing my thesis, I have moved from leadership in the Centre into full-time teaching in Saint Paul University's Master of Pastoral Theology and Doctor of Ministry programs. I continue to use and study this immunity-to-change language form with students and communities. These experiences deepen my conviction that leaders have a responsibility to help people move "beyond the edge of familiar patterns into the unknown territory of greater complexity."[11] Language can facilitate new learning and new structures for understanding that can lead to new behaviours and practices.

This book is addressed to individuals and facilitators who are interested in discovering ways of seeing and becoming a more inclusive church. It is my hope that people in pastoral leadership roles, including educators for pastoral ministry and those who accompany pastoral leaders in their growth and continuing education, will find this a useful resource for addressing the challenges of leading and educating for change. This book does not assume anything about your own commitment to change, except that you are truly committed to expanding your current vision and practice of ministry. It does, however, presuppose the following: your vision of church embraces the dynamism of the Spirit of the Risen Christ, who calls us to participate in God's mission in this world as it unfolds; you are committed to personal change in your own ways of ministering and being more inclusive; and you have encountered resistance to moving beyond exclusive practices in your own ministry and in the ministry of your church and community.

Outline of the book

Throughout this book, I invite you to try on new languages I have chosen to expand our ways of seeing and being church. Each chapter incorporates and builds on the story and language presented in previous chapters.

Chapter 1 lays the foundation for engaging in the process of change, both individually and collectively. Chapter 2 tells the story of both my personal and ministerial context in a way that visibly connects my personal story with my ministry and my research on language and change. My aim in Chapter 2 is to inspire you to examine your own stories of ministry to gain wisdom from your journey and the visions that animate your ministry. My own story, as well as my focus on the relationship between language and change, has influenced my choice of theoretical and theological frameworks, as explored in the subsequent chapters.

Chapters 3, 4 and 5 are theoretical and speculative. As you read through them, I invite you to be aware of the questions and issues you bring to the texts I have chosen. In Chapter 3, I propose a theoretical framework based on evolutionary and feminist thought. Here I draw on five concepts—energy, consciousness, story, praxis, and system—that together offer a lens for viewing reality. My choice of this theoretical model recognizes the significant impact that evolutionary and feminist thought have had on social and cultural transformations. Both types of thought continue to shape our ways of thinking and acting. This same theoretical model provides a hermeneutical lens for critically retrieving and reconstructing elements of our Trinitarian doctrine and ecclesial vision. It also offers a conceptual basis for the "immunity-to-change language technology," including its psychological underpinnings.

Chapter 4 rests on the conviction that our God image is the ultimate reference point for the values of all Christian communities.[12] In this chapter, I propose elements of the theology of the relationships within the Triune God to give us a fundamental basis for critically reflecting on our ministerial and ecclesial praxis. By retrieving the ancient language of *perichoresis* and *koinonia*, we reaffirm our deep interconnectedness in God with all of creation.

In Chapter 5, I examine two discipleship models of church, both of which propose language that honours the dynamism of the church's movement toward the fullness of communion. The ancient concepts of *ekklesia* and *basileia* remind us that ministry is the fundamental vocation of all the baptized. The new language of holarchy invites us to imagine and choose other ways of seeing and being church today.

Chapter 6 focuses on the "immunity-to-change language technology." In order to provide a theoretical basis for this language form, I offer elements of constructive-development theory and object-relations theory, which explain the dynamic process of human development—both individually and collectively—in relation to our environment. I then lead readers through the four-column exercise that is designed to surface the assumptions that underlie what Kegan and Lahey call our "competing commitments to change." (In the appendices, you will find practical guidelines for facilitating the diagnostic and follow-up phases of this developmental process.)

In the conclusion, I look at our liturgy as a space for consciousness-raising and offer some concluding reflections on the potential of the "immunity-to-change language technology" to free us from our hidden resistance to change.

This book proposes a way for Christians to become freer in living out our mission as disciples of Jesus Christ in the world today. It does not guarantee results. To do so would be to undermine the complexity of the human person, our communities, our church, and the world. In my own life, I have found that there is no quick way to achieve the kind of change this age demands. Over time, I have come to appreciate that we cannot approach the question of change as disengaged researchers. One of the twentieth century's best-known agents of change, Mahatma Gandhi, practised this truth. Gandhi offers us timeless wisdom to guide this exploration of language and change. To become agents of change, we must first change ourselves.

1

Language and Change: Laying the Foundation

Language shapes us and the world in which we live. Because of its deeply formative nature, language can propose and reinforce values and ideals. It can maintain the status quo or it can be a vital means for change. The word *change* evokes a number of images and reactions. The type of change I address in this book is change that moves us toward becoming more fully the people and faith communities that God calls us to be today.

Irenaeus, a well-respected second-century theologian, captured the essence of our Christian heritage with the pithy phrase "The glory of God is the human person fully alive." This truth has echoed through the ages. "Everything that promotes the fullness of humanity [and] that builds up relationships based on charity and compassion, glorifies God."[13] God invites all of humanity into the fullness of life. Baptized Christians hear and respond to this invitation as a call to discipleship. Our response is lived out in relationship within the Body of Christ and with the Risen Christ, with whom we share the ongoing mission of making the reign of God present in our own place and time. Discipleship is marked by ongoing conversion into God's call to share responsibility for the humanization of the world. Humanization is the fundamental vocation of all human beings.[14] The call to develop into the fullness of our humanity is extended to all humans, individually and collectively. When we receive this call to freely choose and act in our journey of growth toward wholeness as gift not only for ourselves, but also for the sake of the world, both we as individuals and the world cannot remain unchanged.[15]

Two kinds of language for change

Scripture tells us that Jesus realized his mission through word and deed. New ideas led to new ways of speaking, which led to new ways of acting and of seeking life in God. The language we use to articulate our Christian stories and doctrine shapes the way we understand our tradition and life as Christians today.[16] Our language can either enable or disable us—individually and as church—from freely engaging in the journey toward wholeness.

In holding up language as a means for change, I distinguish between two kinds of language: the language of content, or *what* we speak, and the language of form, or *how* we speak. Both can enable change. Throughout this book, I intentionally use words to express *what* we know of God, church, humanity, and world that reflect my inclusive and dynamic view of reality. As a socio-historical body, the church influences and is affected by the many developments in both the natural and human sciences. Strands of evolutionary and feminist thought are making their way into our ways of seeing and being church, offering fresh ways of perceiving and naming reality. For example, language that expresses the immanence of God can move us to see and respond with more clarity to God's gracious presence in our daily lives. Contemporary terms such as *energy*, *consciousness*, *story*, *praxis*, and *system* provide a lens through which to critically retrieve and reinterpret ancient Christian concepts such as *koinonia*, *perichoresis*, *ekklesia*, and *basileia*. These concepts, which we will explore in detail in Chapter 5, shape the theological and ecclesiological perspectives that are the means and goal of our journey to realize our mission. As we forge a new understanding and practice of church, we must also forge a new vocabulary, a new language to express the dynamic and developmental nature of the pilgrim church. I describe my vision for becoming the church we are called to be in these times as "moving toward a more inclusive church."

The phrase *moving toward* indicates that this model of being church involves an ongoing process. Theologian Rémi Parent captures this idea when he claims that "the church takes on meaning only in those for whom being church is *becoming* church."[17] The process of becoming is not in itself tied to a particular principle, theology, role, person, community, historical period, hierarchy, or institutional structure. However, because the church is a concrete reality, it takes on a particular form based on particular principles, theologies, roles, and structures of its time. Although sharing in Christ's mission remains at the centre of the church's identity, the church's form or way of being church is not permanent. This is evident when we compare our current ecclesial structures to those of the early Christian communities. As I propose in more detail in Chapter 5, the structures of the church have and will continue to change as the church strives to more fully realize its mission as it journeys in this world as a pilgrim church.

Language and inclusivity

Inclusivity is at the core of God's desire for the world. Jesus was constantly attentive to who was missing from the table. The parables of the lost sheep and the lost coin, as well as the healing stories, exemplify his concern for including those who were marginalized by the social and religious norms of the time. The church is always asked to become more inclusive. Each particular time and place calls us to see who is missing from the table. Even Jesus' practice of inclusivity was challenged by the Syrophoenician (in Matthew, Canaanite) woman, who claimed a place in God's realm through the healing of her daughter (Mark 7:25; Matthew 15:21-28). Inclusivity was also a concern of the first Christian communities. Paul's mission to the Gentiles forced the church to rethink its rules and boundaries of membership in the one Body of Christ (Acts 15). Inclusivity has never been a trivial concern for the church; it determines the fundamental relations within the church as well as the church's relationship with the world.

Our practices of inclusivity are not value-neutral. They are directly related to what or whom we consider to be of value (or not). When the first disciples asked Jesus, "Who is the greatest in the kingdom of heaven?" he took a child in his arms, challenging the conventional tendency of his time to marginalize children (Matthew 18:1-5). The same question, "Who is the greatest in the kingdom of heaven?", challenges us to rethink how we practise inclusivity today in our relations within the church as well as between the church and the world. Divorce and remarriage, gay and lesbian couples, the environmental crisis, women's increasing role in church ministry—these and other current realities are calling us to redefine the boundaries we have placed on the extent of God's reach into the world, and challenge the church to rethink how to live its mission inclusively today.

Changing "how" we speak

Language is a significant factor in moving toward a more inclusive church. Change in *what* we speak can open us to the possibility of seeing reality differently. However, this is not enough to make the change necessary for living out our mission today. We cannot "make the significant shifts in perspective and practice"[18] that are required for our time without examining and expanding our forms of knowing.

Changing *how* we speak can enable us to surface hidden assumptions that preserve our current ways of making meaning. Changing how we speak is changing our language form, which can equip us to move beyond our familiar patterns of deciding what is true and real for us. Changing how we speak can open the way for us to engage in the messy work of disturbing a coherent set of unspoken rules that maintain our structures of knowing. This is the work of human development. It forces us to move beyond our comfort zones. The kind of change required for "walking upright," as Jung called it, is arduous work.[19] Yet changing how we speak can help us change our relationship to change itself. It can help us become more aware of our hopes, dreams, and fears, which often remain unspoken yet have a powerful hold on our choices and actions.

In my own research and practice as a pastoral educator, I have found the "immunity-to-change language technology"[20] to be an important resource for changing how we speak. This language form was designed by Harvard developmental educators Robert Kegan and Lisa Laskow Lahey, who presented it in their book *How the Way We Talk Can Change the Way We Work: Seven Languages for Transformation*. The word *work* is usually understood to be what we do as employment or labour. However, there are a multitude of ways in which we use the word *work*: it can mean how we choose and act; it can also refer to "alternating movements with some implication of force exerted against the resistance to act,"[21] such as working the lid of a jar until it is finally pried loose. As you will discover, the "immunity-to-change language technology" is designed to loosen the hold of our resistance to change.

And although the name of this language form is long and somewhat awkward, the terms *immunity* and *technology* are apt. The word *immunity*, which is a biological term that we normally associate with our physical well-being, captures our inherent human preference for stability and self-preservation. This language form is built on the conviction that we all have some degree of immunity to change. In other words, it is perfectly natural for all humans and all human organizations, including the church, to carry a simultaneous commitment to change and non-change. The term *technology*, reflecting its Greek root, *techne,* "suggests the artful or skillful activity of making or building."[22] As a tool for building or constructing meaning, the "immunity-to-change language technology" can help us develop our capacity to reflect, discern, and act more responsibly. The more we develop our abilities to make meaning of our world and mission, the better equipped we will be to live as Christians today.

Language and meaning-making

The "immunity-to-change language technology" is also based on the premise that we as humans all have a fundamental need to make meaning of our experiences. The meaning-making process is a basic element of all human development, both individually and collectively. We make meaning of our outer and inner experiences through frames of reference that we call *mental structures*. They work as systems, each with their own inner logic, to regulate our thinking (cognitive) and feeling (affective), as well as social dynamics.[23] Whether or not we are even conscious of our own meaning systems, the process of meaning-making is in itself value-laden. Those values are influenced by a number of factors, including the events and relationships in our families and communities of origin, religion and culture, as well as our unique personalities. In a constructivist approach to human development, meaning-making is not a one-time event. Rather, it is an ongoing process marked by continuous movement between autonomy and inclusion into higher, more complex, and inclusive orders of consciousness.[24] I will elaborate on this development process and the concept of mental structure in Chapter 6.

We generally make meaning by integrating new experiences into what we already know. However, new experiences and new information can challenge our existing frames of reference. To avoid the chaos of the unknown, we may choose, consciously or unconsciously, to ignore what is new and try to fit the experience into what we already know. Or, we can use our new experiences to call into question our current ways of knowing. Over the last century, significant events and crises have forced us to examine and change our meaning-making structures.

These events include two world wars; wars fought in Asia and the Middle East; genocides, such as those in Bosnia, Rwanda and Sudan; the current ecological crisis; the gigantic leaps in technology; the liberation movements; and the rise of feminism. The issues and questions arising from these events do not fit into our familiar ways of knowing.

In moving toward a more inclusive church, we hear and respond to the call for change in our current ways of knowing and making meaning of our experiences. This ecclesial vision is based on the conviction that as our consciousness develops and becomes more complex so does our ability to imagine genuine possibilities for living as church today.[25] Imagination is the power to form or define new ideas, either by combining or considering separate elements of an experience. Our tradition shows that Christian life is incomplete without imagination. Jesus' parables and metaphorical language—the mustard seed, the talents, the eye of the needle—engage our imagination and help us find ways to live out the challenges of faithful discipleship today. In my ministry as a practical theologian, Jesus' call to "put out into the deep" (Luke 5:1-11) fuels my imagination when devising learning opportunities that enable learners to muster the courage and confidence to leave the comfort of the shoreline and move out into the depths of reality. Without imagination, we remain caught in a cycle of patterns that undermine our journey of growth toward wholeness. The language we intentionally choose can allow us to imagine new ways of seeing and being church today. The "immunity-to-change language technology" can help us develop more complex structures of meaning and imagine genuine possibilities for exercising our mission as Christians today.

Types of change

Change is a very broad term expressing what we experience in our journey of growth throughout our lives. I offer three ways to consider change, all of which are part of our human development into wholeness. The first makes a distinction between informational and transformational change. The second looks at whether change is emergent or intentional. The third deals with the pace of change, whether it is incremental or episodic. Often, the three overlap or interconnect.

Change can be informational or transformational. Informational change is change in *what* we know; transformational change is change in *how* we know. As we acquire knowledge, skills, and competencies throughout our lives, some of them fit into our current meaning structures and others call our frames of reference into question. Transformational change occurs when the "form" of our knowing is disturbed. Although transformational change includes change in what we as individuals and organizations know, it is not possible to undergo this type of change without experiencing a shift in our assumptions. Assumptions make up our systems of meaning that consciously or unconsciously affect our choices and behaviours. Transformational change is deep structural change, change in our mental structures.

Change can be emergent or intentional. Emergent change occurs in an unplanned way. We have all had experiences of unplanned change: the sudden death of someone close to us, a new relationship, a move to another place for a job, for example. Intentional change is purposeful, the result of conscious reasoning, choices, and actions—a new job, marriage, even retirement. However, even the best-planned lives are peppered with emergent change, which can surprise us and cause us to deviate from our original plans. Seasoned parents know that they can intentionally strive to acquire and use good parenting skills, but also know that the most important lessons children learn come from the unplanned incidents in life.

Change can be incremental or episodic. Incremental change is continuous and cumulative change. As we develop in our personal and professional lives, we build on previous knowledge and skills step by step. We incorporate what we learn into our mental structures. Eventually, the cumulative effect of continuous adjustments can lead to transformational change. Episodic change, on the other hand, often involves isolated events, such as the death of a loved one, a mid-life crisis, a job loss, or falling in love. This kind of change takes us away from what we know. Unexpectedly, and in some cases very suddenly, our new experiences no longer fit into our current mental structures.

Changing our language can be a way to enable intentional change that is both informational and transformational, incremental and episodic. For example, as we intentionally speak a new language to express a more expansive view of God, the church, humanity, and the world, we gradually open ourselves to seeing a more inclusive and dynamic view of reality. However, while change in what we speak can eventually contribute to transforming our ways of being church, any kind of change risks remaining superficial if we do not examine and transform our assumptions through which we make meaning and determine truth. The "immunity-to-change language technology" is an important resource for helping us do this demanding yet necessary work for living out our Christian mission today.

Language and change in the Second Vatican Council

The church has a long history of summoning councils to deal with significant issues related to change. In its historical development, the Roman Catholic Church has had five major councils, beginning with the Council of Jerusalem in the first century and ending with the Second Vatican Council in the 1960s. While each of those councils was concerned with issues particular to its time and place, all of them addressed the question of change—specifically, how institutions live incremental and episodic change in their own place and time.[26] The Second Vatican Council reveals that no council takes place in a void. Although the Second Vatican Council triggered a period of episodic change, it was preceded by years of incremental change in the church and the socio-historical context. Before Pope John XXIII made the radical decision to call the council, many changes in the church and world had already taken place. The Second World War, as well as the pre- and post-war periods, played a pivotal role in leading people to call into question their theological frameworks for making meaning of reality. The church could no longer ignore the growing demands of modernity, with its defining marks of democracy, technology, autonomy, and human rights.

Almost 50 years later, the change continues. We now live in a time often referred to as "postmodernity," in which the modern myth of progress has given way to the reality of globalization, plurality, and ecology. Just as individuals cannot remain the same, all human institutions are in constant need of change to continue to be faithful to their mission. As a human institution, the church continues to heed the call to change in order to be faithful to its fundamental mission of transforming and humanizing the world. As the church journeys into change, language plays an important role in the process.

The Second Vatican Council chose the language of *ressourcement* and *aggiornamento* to guide the church's rediscovery of its mission. *Ressourcement* signals the call to return to our theological and ecclesiological sources to rediscover the core of our identity. *Aggiornamento* signals the call to engage in the process of modernization—a journey of renewal and reconstruction in which we update and expand what we already know in order to be faithful to our present and future calling. This journey of renewal is transformational change. This depth of change is not possible without our returning to our sources, in critical dialogue with the particular questions of our time.

Change shaped by the language of *ressourcement* and *aggiornamento* is not directed by personal whim or passing cultural fads. It is guided by the Spirit of the Risen Christ, who is both "catalyst and agent" of the church's continuous renewal and reformation.[27] The same Spirit that inspired the early Christians more than 2,000 years ago to live out their mission in critical dialogue with the issues of their place and time is active today. This kind of transformational change requires a shift in the assumptions that keep us from becoming the church we are called to be in these times. Our language can help us make that shift by transforming our ways of reading the signs and discerning the reality of our times.

Conclusion

My experience continues to show me the importance of addressing this issue of language and change. It was in the context of my work at the Centre for Ministry Formation at Saint Paul University that I first became convinced that change in both what and how we speak can enable change in the church. However, although I was attentive to speaking an inclusive and invitational language, I realized that just doing that was not enough to allow me to make the leap that such transformational change required. My work with the "immunity-to-change language technology" has shown me that until we bring to the fore assumptions that anchor our immunity to change, we are working against the prospect of actually moving toward a more inclusive church. This language form opens up new possibilities for change when we can appreciate how hard it is to truly overcome resistance to change, especially when our resistance is subconscious.

Like you, I too have a personal history that has brought me to where I live out my mission today. My history is interconnected with my family, community, and culture, as well as the many facets of the environment in which I currently minister. As a member of the Roman Catholic Church and as an educator in ministry formation and pastoral leadership in a Roman Catholic university, I am immersed in a culture that is often immune to change. As I carry out my responsibilities for forming lay and ordained ministers, I live the challenges of this immunity to change in myself, in others, and in the church.

I have come to appreciate that each of us views "theology and our understanding of how God is at work in our lives, through a particular lens of language, thought and action."[28] I reflect on my experience from my own location. In my case, I am a woman in a pastoral leadership role in the Roman Catholic Church in Canada. From that perspective, I ask questions, make claims, and use theories and language that reflect my location, some of which do not align with those of other people who minister in my faith community. It is because of this experience that I believe language can help us work through our immunity to change and become more responsible in exercising our mission as church today.

2

Telling the Story

The way we tell a story depends on the message we want to convey. I have chosen to tell my story as well as the story of ministry formation at Saint Paul University through the lens of discipleship and change. I hope that these stories will reflect some of the patterns in your own story and quest for realizing your commitments to change in living your own mission.

My story

My story is marked by a number of changes in close relationships, church membership, and career path. Some changes were planned; others were not. Some were incremental, while some involved major shifts in my ways of seeing and being in the world. As all personal stories do, mine features specific rules and events that shaped me.

When I was a child, the steadfast rule of "family first" made it difficult for me to fit in with other groups. Self-importance was discouraged, so it was hard for me to speak out of my own experience. My primary and high school education in the English Protestant system in suburban Quebec was marked by benevolence, paternalism, and monarchy. The daily ritual of reciting the Lord's Prayer and the Lord is My Shepherd (King James Version) and of singing "God Save the Queen" was deeply formative. When I was twelve years old, my mother died of breast cancer. That event triggered a number of changes for my family and me. I continue to wrestle with the effect of my mother's premature death in shaping my sense of self as well as my ways of relating to others.

As a result of my experience of abandonment, which I never spoke of, I had unconsciously been engulfed and driven by fear and anger, which manifested themselves in self-discipline and self-control. This was especially evident in my roles of wife and mother; my need to maintain control and perfect order included controlling my husband and two children. I worked hard at having a perfect family and, in some ways, succeeded. My husband and children can witness to how relentless I was in accomplishing that goal. Our culture rewards us for perfection, even when it is achieved through obsessive or self-defeating behaviours. I know this to be true for the church when it comes to perfect families. When my children were pre-teens and I still had control over them, we received the Knights of Columbus Family of the Year Award. Although I value the intent of an award that seemed right for us at that time, I now see it differently. As I moved into my late 30s, I started noticing what could now be described as the obsessive tendencies that were keeping my family and me from freely acting and choosing. When my son was 15, he gave me a wake-up call: "Mom," he said, "you know what your problem is? You want a perfect family and you will never have one."

That was one of several awakenings at that time of my life. Another occurred when I was praying late one evening. I was quietly reflecting as I prepared to celebrate the Sacrament of Reconciliation as part of a spiritual renewal program in my local parish. Suddenly, I felt a surge of energy through my body. I heard a voice within me ask, "Why are you angry with me?" This question brought an immediate flood of tears as I realized how my anger—at God, myself, and others—was keeping me from living the life to which God was calling me. What I experienced in this holy encounter was pivotal in my journey into freedom and fullness of life. I had learned early in life to ignore and silence my anger. Many of us—especially women—feel out of control and guilty when we are angry, so we ignore our anger in order to preserve our relationships. Furthermore, our religious culture judges anger, at God, above all, as sinful. Yet, "when all anger is condemned as sin, we lose the grace and power that come from anger that is acknowledged and integrated."[29] In that holy encounter, I began my journey of looking *at* my anger rather than *through* it. I began to be pried loose from its control.

Confronting and transforming the energy of our anger is a key part of our becoming more fully who God calls us to be.[30] Yet, the change to which God was calling me was not instantaneous; it is a lifelong journey. Although I was truly committed to realizing that call to fullness of life, my actions revealed my incessant need for control and order. With the support and challenge of those who accompany me in my personal and spiritual growth, and the sometimes not-so-gentle nudges of those closest to me, I came to see how my behaviour and sense of self were being unconsciously driven by fears and assumptions that kept me from the kind of life to which I had a sense God was calling me. As I encountered God's unconditional love, I gradually learned to trust and open up to the surprises that life presents. That change was not without some pain as I let go of some of my familiar patterns of acting and framing reality. I realized that my self-worth was not in being a supermom who constantly rescued her family, school, community, business, and church from the woes of unfulfilled needs and wants. I did not have to use all my energy to try to make myself and the world around me perfect.

I remember that period of intense change in my life as a time when I began to truly hear the call to discipleship. Jesus' call to "Follow me!" came in the midst of a very busy life, with a family and a family business to manage. That call to follow Christ was not a call to flee or leave behind my life commitments. Rather, it was about carrying, integrating, and transforming those commitments in response to what I was beginning to understand as an invitation to participate in Christ's mission in the world. In my eagerness to respond, I became actively engaged in pastoral and social ministries, as well as faith-sharing groups, in which I tried to make meaning of what I was living. I began seeing others and relationships in a different light, as I was gradually becoming freed from my need to control my environment.

As I gained a deeper trust in and closer relationship with God, I found myself praying for two gifts in particular. The first was the gift of discernment. I had experienced an intense desire to pay attention to God's presence in my life and in the world. I knew that greater attentiveness would allow me to become a little wiser and a little freer in the choices I make. As theologian Patricia O'Connell Killen states, "without desire we do not receive; yet, our desiring can be skewed, off the mark, or blocked in ways that interfere with receiving what we seek most clearly."[31] I know this to be true in my own life. As I tell and reflect on my story, it becomes clearer to me that there is no other route to receiving the gift of wisdom than practising a faith that "does not fear the ambiguous spaces in ourselves and in our world where death and life are intimately connected."[32]

The second gift I prayed for was language. I had felt a call to become better at both listening and speaking about what I had seen, heard, discerned, and done. I began to feel a sense of kinship and desire to accompany others as they pursued their own paths into freedom. Our Christian heritage reminds us that all gifts are offered not only for ourselves but also for the good of the community. As believers, we are all called to receive gifts and integrate them into our lives. In doing so, I decided to offer them in service of those seeking greater freedom to live out their particular mission toward the fullness of life.

With my new awareness, and being convinced of my call to discipleship, I gradually became more and more involved in the life and mission of the church. My pastor asked me to attend a five-day institute on the Christian initiation of children. That experience triggered for me a series of episodic changes in my personal growth and what I was coming to understand as vocational discernment. That five-day institute opened the door to several years of theological studies and to more service in the local church, which eventually led me to ministry as a pastoral educator at Saint Paul University. As my itinerary shows, both the individual and the world, including the institution in which we serve, are affected by our journey toward wholeness.

We each hear and discern Jesus' call to discipleship in different ways. One of the ways I heard it was in the form of an invitation by my pastor to consider part-time parish ministry, in which he cited this Scripture passage:

> But you are a chosen race, a royal priesthood, a holy nation, God's own people, in order that you may proclaim the mighty acts of him who called you out of darkness into his marvelous light. (1 Peter 2:9)

He knew my story; he knew I had indeed been called out of darkness by walking into the darkness of my own fears and assumptions. The best way I can describe my experience of call and response at that time is that I had a sense of being catapulted into very deep change. My response to that call to discipleship was to serve in my parish and diocesan church, and to pursue studies in theology, all of which changed me.

I have now come to appreciate even more acutely that we cannot disconnect personal change from institutional change. This truth was especially evident for me from 1999 to 2005, when I served as director of the Centre for Ministry Formation at Saint Paul University. It was during that time that I did my initial research on people's immunity to change. In collaboration with a team of pastoral educators, I was responsible for developing and delivering the Centre's ministry formation and vocational discernment process for people who presented themselves as candidates for ordained and lay ministry. Although the candidates are mainly members of the Roman Catholic Church, the Centre welcomes individuals from other Christian traditions as well. Now, as a professor in the Master of Pastoral Theology and Doctor of Ministry programs, which are shaped by this same ecclesial vision, I continue to journey with adult learners who are preparing for or already engaged in some form of ministry. They, too, are changing how they engage in ministry and in their relationship to their respective institutions.

Family history plays a unique role in ministry. It also influences research interests. In my case, the pain of unresolved incidents of clergy control and sexual abuse severed my ancestral roots in the Roman Catholic Church. In his early 30s, my paternal grandfather stormed out of the Roman Catholic Church, taking his whole family with him. One of his sisters had been raped by a priest. When my grandfather confronted the priest about the abuse, she was blamed for the incident. The priest had the last word: he was right; my grandfather was wrong. This all took place in 1930s Quebec, when the demarcation between the French and English culture was accentuated by the deep division between Protestants and Catholics. As an ex-Roman Catholic francophone, my father was deeply marked by the agony of exclusion. Unknowingly, I carried his pain and the unfulfilled, very human need to belong. Although my grandfather chose never to share the details of that story, even with his own family, those unspoken events shaped my ecclesiology, my theology and my identity as a pastoral minister.

As a result of this family history, I was baptized in the Anglican Church and spent my early years in the anglophone United Church. After I was married, I experienced a tentative and gradual immersion into a francophone Roman Catholic community with my husband. Only after several years of being on the periphery did I choose to enter into full communion with the Roman Catholic Church in an anglophone community. "It's time to come full circle": these were the exact words I used to express what I was feeling when I met with the pastor of what had become our family's faith community. Somehow, I knew it was time for me to choose to be included in this particular church. What I did not know was that this choice was also moving me into a time of deep change—a time in which I would become aware of how my early formation had marked my own development and choices. At that time, I was unaware of the reason for my grandfather's rupture with the Roman Catholic Church. My grandfather, who was still alive at that time, grimly accepted my decision and vowed never to discuss it with me. Two months after my grandfather died, the pastor of the parish that embraced me as a full member of the community was convicted of sexual abuse. It was only then that my aunt shared some of my grandfather's story with me. Over time, I have come to see how my family's unspoken story had fuelled my conviction that ministry formation and pastoral leadership education must be a journey of growth toward wholeness and authentic claiming of our identities as subjects who freely relate with others as subjects of their own lives.

My personal core convictions

All these events have been formative for me and for those with whom I journey. In my attempts to make meaning of my experiences, I have become clearer about the core convictions that are foundational to my ministry. My first core conviction is that all change is guided either consciously or unconsciously by a value system. In naming our value system, we have the opportunity to transform it and claim it as our own. For me, interdependence, inclusivity, and integration are three fundamental values for Christian discipleship in these complex times. As I reflect on my story, I can see how these three values guide change in my life. Interdependence is mutual dependence; each person is both independent from and in relationship with the other. I have come to adopt interdependence as a way of living and to recognize I am one among many. Like all people, I must trust and rely on the support and challenge of others in order to realize my mission. As an interdependent minister and educator, I recognize the incompleteness of my own gifts and systems of meaning. The call to interdependence heightens my awareness that I have blind spots that keep me from seeing reality as others do. I have come to see that I am called to freely accept my own gifts and limits, as well as the gifts and limits of others.

Inclusivity shapes my way of knowing and acting. I consider hospitality to be an act of inclusivity when we stand with others without judgment as both host and guest, enabling them to hear the Spirit in their own lives, as they become more fully who they are called to be. Inclusivity causes us to spiral between the centre and the margins, seeking out the excluded and challenging our conventional norms for determining legitimate diversity. Inclusivity holds together the divisive categories of them and us, body and spirit, doing and being, essence and energy, mind and emotions as we develop more complex ways of knowing so that we can interpret reality. Whenever we transcend the dualistic practices of exclusivism, sexism, classicism, elitism, and clericalism, we practise inclusivity.

Integration is a distinctively human activity that stems from our capacity to adapt to reality "*plus* the critical capacity to make choices and to transform that reality."[33] If we are incapable of changing that reality, then we simply adapt ourselves and adjust as objects to external prescriptions imposed on us. In contrast, the integrated person can make choices and therefore is a subject who is capable of changing reality. Integration is wholeness, a quality of life for which all humans strive. The complexity of the times in which we live can leave us fragmented, disconnected, and incapable of making responsible choices. When we engage in the liberating work of bringing together contradictory elements of ourselves and our environments, we increase our capacity to live into the fullness of our humanity. However, it is an illusion to think that we will ever fully embrace any of our cherished values. As I continue my lifelong journey of critically integrating my personal history into my current ways of living, I catch myself at times contradicting my values and commitments. This is most apparent in the ways I defend my boundaries and strive to control situations when I experience loss, fear, or uncertainty.

My second core conviction is that women have a responsibility to speak from their location and tell the stories of their call to discipleship and their ministry. It is still a challenge for me to tell my story. Over several years of pastoral practice and theological studies, I had unwittingly convinced myself that it was safer to speak from a theoretical stance so that I could remain neutral. I was unequipped to face some of my own experiences of exclusionary practices in the Roman Catholic Church. I have come to see that neutrality renders us dispassionate and detached. Only in being confronted with the pain of those experiences and the fear of exposing my struggle have I come to realize that I cannot avoid naming the experience. In remaining silent,

I acquiesced to the theories and structures that are the very source of legitimation of those exclusionary practices. Not only are women impoverished when women choose to be silent but so also is the church. The lack of women role models supports the sparse historical evidence of women's contribution to the evolution of church and culture.

A critical reflection on elements of my own story has enabled me to see that the passion of my own life and my commitment to the lives of others have led me to identify the theological issues of greatest concern to me. This critical reflection has helped me develop greater awareness of my own world views, assumptions, and frames of reference through which I make meaning of my experience. In my ministry, I have the privilege of accompanying and hearing the stories of various people who seek to discern their call to discipleship. Here, I experience "simultaneous desire and disillusionment"[34] as I both rejoice in the generosity with which they respond to God's call and struggle with the exclusionary structures of our chosen faith community, which confine ordained ministry to the celibate male.[35] Our narrow vision blinds us from recognizing the Spirit's call to try on new ways of seeing and being church in these times. In the midst of this struggle, I fervently work at carefully articulating my questions and deep-seated desire for transformation of structures and practices. This struggle is both the source and goal of my fascination and passion for sharing and deepening what I have come to know about how language can enable change.

My third core conviction is that I cannot do this challenging work of transformation alone. I have and continue to contend with my assumption that if I am perceived as being angry or frustrated, I will not be taken seriously as a woman in ministry in the Roman Catholic Church. In living with this tension, I have found allies in some of my colleagues, both within and outside my university community, who support me and help me resist self-deception. Over time, I have found myself drawn to standing with those who seek the affirmation and promotion of the full humanity of women, men, and children. My gradual conversion to feminist thought was not without some hesitation and pain. My painful initiation took place in the early 1970s in a course on feminist thought at a Quebec community college. There I was introduced to the caustic edge to feminism. The first book on the syllabus was *I B.I.T.C.H.* (I, Ball-breaker Intend To Castrate Him.)[36] I never finished that course. I confronted a world view that was so foreign and threatening to me at the time that my only recourse was to reject it outright. Since that time, I have come to see that all counter-positions to societal norms go through a number of stages in their development. This was true for feminism. *I B.I.T.C.H.* was a manifesto for female liberation written in the early stages of the feminist movement.

I, too, have gone through a number of changes that have led me to selectively embrace feminist convictions today. Now deeply inspired by the courage and wisdom of reformist feminist theologians, I have come to recognize that a faith community shapes its God-language to express its view of the world and that order flows from that view. As I explore and speak from within the Roman Catholic tradition, I stand with other Christian reformist feminist theologians who have not given up on the church's capacity to be inclusive of people on the margins. And with other reformist feminist theologians, I struggle with the transformation of the life-giving, liberating nature of Christian language and symbols so that all may freely respond to God's call to fullness of life. These convictions flow from and shape my life, ministry, and relationship with God. I work through the theological issues that are of great concern to me through the agony and passion of my life and my commitment to the lives of others.[37]

When I consider my story as well as the stories of those I accompany in light of Carl Jung's vivid claim that we can either walk upright or be dragged through life,[38] I see the Spirit calling us into the development needed in our time. I also see more clearly how our immunity to change keeps us from responding to that very call. I now turn to the story of the Centre for Ministry Formation, a story that, like my story, is characterized by a complex web of events, ideas, and conditions.

The story of ministry formation at Saint Paul University

Any change in the church requires change in the way we form ministers and pastoral leaders. The story of my context of ministry shows how both go hand in hand. The official origin of ministry formation at Saint Paul University goes back to 1937, when its seminary opened its doors and welcomed seminarians from several dioceses across Canada and the United States, as well as from a number of male religious communities. As with my personal history, Saint Paul University's history of ministry formation has been marked by both incremental and episodic change. The history of change can be divided into four ages of episodic change, each of which is marked by a particular vision of church and ministry,[39] and each of which continues to be incorporated, at times unknowingly, into our current ministry formation process.

The first age spanned from the seminary's opening to the Second Vatican Council in the mid-1960s. For about 35 years, the rule of seminary life was to "provide regularity, observance of its religious obligations, and an orderly Seminary life in accordance with the directives of the Holy See and Seminary discipline."[40] The overall purpose of the rule was to foster inner freedom, confidence, sanctity, and a solid doctrinal formation. The rule not only shaped the formation community of that age but also reflected the prevailing vision of church and ministry, which was characterized by order, regularity and strict observance of religious obligations within a monastic setting in which the seminarians had little or no contact with the outside world.

The second age was ushered in by the Second Vatican Council's burning desire for renewal beginning in the second half of the 1960s. This desire for change carried with it a vision of church and ministry that no longer fit the rule of the first age. Given the profundity of the changes immediately following the council, the turmoil of the second age was inevitable. The disorienting experience of instability was symbolic of what was happening at every level of church life. Not only was there a drastic drop in the number of candidates for ordained ministry in seminaries across the country but there was also a mass exodus from religious communities and presbyteral ministry. This radical decline was also experienced at Sunday Mass, particularly in francophone communities in Quebec. Without the familiar framework in which church members had forged their identity and practice, many experienced a deep loss and were disoriented. Many members of the clergy, religious communities, and the laity chose to abandon a way of life that had lost both its power over them and its capacity to speak to them at the core of their being. Saint Paul University Seminary was no exception to this radical decline. The number of seminarians fell by more than half in just a few years, from 120 in the mid-60s to 53 in 1971. In this time of intense change, the rule of the first age, with its vision of church and ministry, no longer spoke to the aspirations of the candidates or the needs of the Canadian church.[41]

For some, this degree of upheaval is difficult to understand. Institutions are generally associated with unchanging tradition—rarely with innovation. When institutions choose to innovate, be it on the macro-level such as the Second Vatican Council, or on the micro-level such as at Saint Paul Seminary, they create a tension between tradition and innovation. When members experience that tension as being threatening or chaotic, they may choose to reject it and walk away, seeking the solace of more familiar ways of defining what is real and true. The story of ministry formation in Saint Paul University witnesses to the immense challenges we all face, as individuals and as church, in our attempts to live in the tension between tradition and innovation in a way that is creative, life-giving, and deeply attentive to the Spirit guiding us to change.

The third age began when the rule of the seminary was updated in 1971 in the spirit of the Second Vatican Council. While traditional structures, such as spiritual direction, initiation to prayer, daily Eucharist and the Office, were preserved, other elements were added to foster social and personal development. These elements signalled an intentional shift in relations, not only within the seminary but also between the seminary and the outside world. The Second Vatican Council had called the church to turn to the world. Until this time, there had been a very clear demarcation between the church as sacred and the world as secular. Now, pastoral activities were being intentionally designed to encourage seminarians to remain in contact with the world during their theological studies and ministry formation.

While the regularity and order of the daily devotions were not dismissed, there was a move toward basing seminary formation on principles of adult education. This is evident in the opportunity seminarians were given to have input into the overall program they would follow, the decisions they would make about their involvement in some of their formation activities and how they would be evaluated. Seminarians took part in faith-sharing groups in which together they sought to make meaning of their experiences of God in their lives and ministry. A student council was established to help create and promote dialogue between the seminary staff and the seminarians. Committees of seminarians took on responsibilities in the community. The seminary staff developed a more elaborate evaluation procedure to involve the student in self-evaluation and feedback. These were the major innovations of this climate shift toward mutual confidence.[42]

The defining vision of the third age was expressed in the language of co-responsibility and empowerment. This was the beginning of an understanding of ministry formation as a dynamic process in which the whole community shared in the search and construction of truth. In this "rule" of the third age, the vision of church and ministry was characterized by the movement from a childlike dependence on order, obligation, and outer authority toward a more adult, independent stance of co-responsibility and empowerment for both the ordained and the laity. In this age, the vision of ministry and church was less triumphant and involved more dialogue with others outside the boundaries it had defined for itself than had previously been the case.

The transition into the fourth age started with the opening of the Centre for Ministry Formation in 1997. As the role of laity in the church increased, Saint Paul University recognized the growing need to prepare lay pastoral associates for ecclesial ministry. Rather than provide a separate formation track for lay ministers, the university decided to launch the Centre to offer formation for candidates for both lay and ordained ministries. The university was careful to maintain the tension between tradition and innovation by maintaining the seminary's status as a separate entity in order to meet the requirements of canon law and the norms of the Canadian Conference of Catholic Bishops but at the same time having seminarians engaged in formation at the Centre for Ministry Formation.[43] In the newly formed structure, the leadership of the Centre was provided by its director in collaboration with the associate director for lay ministries and associate director for ordained ministries, who was also rector of the seminary. When the Centre opened in 1997, it welcomed eleven candidates for ordained ministry and its first candidate for lay ministry, a woman named Louise Auclair.[44] Louise was soon to be followed by other women and men seeking a place for vocational discernment and preparation for ministry. This age marks the development of a visibly new vision of church and ministry—a vision that first attracted me to ministry in the Centre itself. This same vision fostered my own identity as disciple and sparked my imagination for future possibilities for our church.

The Centre's core convictions

The Centre's ecclesial vision of change is based on three core convictions, all of which underline its faithfulness to the Second Vatican Council's call to *ressourcement* and *aggiornamento*.

First, the centre is an agent of transformation in its own ecclesial culture, since it incorporates both tradition and innovation into its ministry formation process. It reorganizes, builds on, and changes the developing story of ministry formation and pastoral leadership education at Saint Paul University. Because the Centre forms ministers who will take leadership roles in their respective communities, it is also an agent of transformation of the larger ecclesial culture, since these ministers will influence the ecclesial environment in which they minister. The Centre recognizes that while the development of particular skills and competencies for ministry is essential, it is not enough. Pastoral leadership education must also provide transformative learning opportunities for shaping candidates' attitudes and identities as collaborative, interdependent, integrated, and transformative pastoral leaders. These qualities are rooted in the renewed vision of church and ministry expressed in the Vatican II documents and in the developing ecclesiologies and theologies that are inspired by those same texts.

Second, the Centre's vision of formation is based on the very broad and multi-faceted model of church as communion in which all the baptized and all ministries are valued. This model of church provides the ecclesiological framework for a community of disciples that lives out its mission in moving toward a more inclusive church. This model of church is the vision that guides the Centre in forming pastoral leaders for collaboration and mutuality. Using language that includes the prefix "co-" encourages candidates for ministry to exercise co-discipleship as co-educators.

Building on the values of co-responsibility and empowerment first named in the vision of the third age, the Centre offers an integral formation process for all candidates for ministry in a community marked by inclusivity, integration, and interdependence. Integral formation includes human, pastoral, spiritual, and intellectual development as prescribed by the guidelines for presbyteral formation.[45] The behaviours and attitudes of an interdependent disciple are the measuring stick for assessing healthy relationships and pastoral practice. Interdependence presupposes and builds on the capacity for both dependence and independence, both of which are critically appropriated and integrated as we journey toward wholeness. As the candidates for ministry support and challenge each other in their personal growth, new relationships emerge and the community of disciples is strengthened.

The third core conviction is related to the first two. The Centre's practice of ministry formation and pastoral leadership education is not simply a series of educational activities designed to achieve an end goal or outcome. Rather, it is praxis. In other words, how it engages in its practice, and how it reflects on its practice, matters. A close look at the Centre's praxis reveals the values and theories that inform it and that, in turn, shape how it accomplishes its mission of preparing pastoral leaders for moving toward a more inclusive church. If the Centre is truly committed to living out of its ecclesial vision, then it cannot afford to be casual or unintentional in its actions or language. Its actions and language make a difference to its effectiveness in forming pastoral leaders to become freer to walk upright in our time.

The challenges and obstacles of living this ecclesial vision are enormous. There is no simple way of engaging in change when moving toward a more inclusive church. Change cannot be legislated. Neither coercion nor censure of exclusive behaviour leads to any serious or long-term change of behaviours and attitudes. It is no easy task to provide an integral formation process that gives equal value to the diversity of ministries for which the candidates present themselves but is also specific to those ministries.

The Centre offers ministry formation in dialogue with the questions and issues of our current context. That formation is intended to move us from the still predominant cleric–lay vision of church to a community–ministries vision in which diverse ministries are called and formally recognized in community in response to the community's needs in fulfilling its mission.[46] This intentional movement has implications for our ministerial praxis as well as our way of living our mission in the world today. As you will read in Chapter 5, the cleric–lay vision of church makes a clear demarcation between the inward-directed ministries, which have been traditionally the domain of the clergy, and outward-directed ministries, which have traditionally been the preserve of the laity. This division keeps the laity dependent upon the clerics and seriously limits laypeople's freedom to choose and act responsibly as church today.

Conclusion

Moving from a cleric–lay vision church is riddled with challenges. The cleric–lay vision of church fosters clericalism and is embedded in a historically rooted philosophical and theological system that perpetuates exclusivist behaviours. While the best of the traditional seminary rules are integrated in the Centre's current praxis, the Centre, like all human organizations, has a simultaneous commitment to change and non-change. The practices that the philosophical and theological system supports counterbalance the Centre's commitment to change, thereby maintaining the status quo. This situation is a real dilemma for the Centre and for any community attempting to live out its authentic commitment to change. Some practices that maintain the status quo are deliberate, while others are unintentional competing commitments of which we are unaware. The "immunity-to-change language technology" addresses the issue of competing commitments for both individuals and community.

In my continuing attempts to make meaning of my own story, along with the ongoing story of my context of ministry, I have discovered that new language can open us to trying on new understandings and new behaviours. New experiences challenge our familiar ways of knowing. In the following chapters, I propose new language for expressing our view of reality—the world, God, church, and humankind.

3

Language and World View: Looking Through a Different Lens

Language is a consciousness-raising activity. When we give voice to our concerns and ideals, they not only exist and are a concern for you or me, but also they express what is real and true for us.[47] There is reciprocal flow between the language we use to express what is real and true, and the framework of ideas and beliefs through which we interpret the world and interact with it. We often refer to this framework as our world view; this is our way of actually experiencing the world. While a contemporary scientific approach to reality tends to either deny or downplay the pervasive influence of religious consciousness on our world view, practical theologians such as Don S. Browning argue that there is a reciprocal flow between our religious consciousness and our world view that shapes our ways of knowing what is real and true. Our world view as well as our religious consciousness have also been deeply shaped by developments in evolutionary and feminist thinking. Both raise questions that concern our time; they offer us a language that allows us to express in a new way, and to rethink how we live our Christian faith in the 21st century. These two types of thought invite us to move from a world view based on domination, competition, and mechanistic thinking toward an inclusive and dynamic view of reality based on the principles of co-creation and interconnectedness. This shift in world view is having an impact on the church's practice as well.

For example, as far back as 1982, the World Council of Churches directed churches to work for "justice, peace and the integrity of creation."[48] This phrase has been integrated into the mission of many congregations of women religious.[49] It also articulates some of the primary concerns of the Canadian Religious Conference (CRC), a network of religious congregations of men and women in Canada that has created and staffed positions to carry out responsibilities in the areas of justice, peace and integrity of creation in all regions of the country. Through the CRC's efforts, ecological concerns as well as justice issues, such as human trafficking and the plight of migrant workers, have received more attention.

Elements of evolutionary thought and feminist thought give us a new language to express what we know and what we desire for ourselves, our church, and our world. From these two very broad fields of inquiry, I draw five concepts: energy, consciousness, story, praxis, and system. While these five words may be familiar, evolutionary and feminist thought build on the standard definitions and offer a more expansive view of reality. I have found these concepts to provide a useful framework for expressing growth in myself and others, as well as the development of organizations, including the church. I invite you to try on this language to see whether it might serve as a framework for understanding your experience and desire for change.

Evolutionary thought: An overview

Our three main companions in this exploration of evolutionary thought are Diarmuid O'Murchu,[50] Cletus Wessels,[51] and Margaret Wheatley.[52] Each of them invites us to see life as a continuous, creative, dynamic process of moving toward greater complexity and inclusivity. Various terms are used to categorize the many strands emerging from evolutionary thought. The strand on which I focus is referred to as the *new cosmology* or the *new science*. O'Murchu and Wessels refer to the former phrase, while Wheatley uses the latter. This fresh vision presents us with concepts, images, and structures that were unknown to previous generations. Both the new cosmology and the new science rely on developing insights in the natural sciences, especially quantum physics, thermodynamics, chemistry, and biology. Both offer us lenses for seeing more clearly the complexity and dynamism of individual and institutional change.

Although most of us may think of Charles Darwin when we hear the word *evolution*, the idea of a gradually unfolding universe goes back to the early Greeks, who understood life as evolving according to universal forms. A historical review of Christian thought shows that for the first 1,600 years of Christianity, the church suppressed the development of any alternative views in favour of a literal interpretation of Genesis that views creation as a one-time event and as retaining its basic structure until the end of time. In contrast to a static view of creation, the theory of evolution presents creation as a process in which life has been evolving over 15 billion years and continues to evolve.[53]

The reasons for the church's suppression of the concept of evolution are multiple and beyond the scope of this book; however, I single out two that are related to our interest in immunity to change. First, ecclesiastical authorities give priority to maintaining stability and order, especially in times of challenge and change. Second, the idea of an external, interventionist God who creates in an orderly and predetermined fashion upholds the church's primary concern for stability and order. An evolutionary view of reality challenges both these approaches.

Scientific discoveries in the sixteenth and seventeenth centuries, mainly by Copernicus, Newton, and Galileo, eventually led, in a series of incremental changes, to a loosening of ecclesiastical control that, in turn, opened the way for a proliferation of research over the subsequent 200 years. In 1859, Charles Darwin published the first treatise associated with the theory of evolution. It offered a radically new view of reality in which randomness, survival, self-preservation, and adaptation were the norm. Although the main tenets of the conventional theory of evolution continue to dominate the Western world view, evolutionary thought has shifted in recent decades to a much larger vision of cosmic and planetary evolution. This vision is often referred to as the new cosmology.

The new cosmology engages our contemporary imagination with respect to our ways of knowing God, humanity, church, and all of creation. It uses language that had been reserved for referring to biological life forms to open the way for a broader understanding of change in human and organizational development. The new cosmology has influenced many strains of evolutionary thought, some of which have been deemed pantheistic or humanistic, giving ultimacy to either the universe or humankind. As we gain a greater appreciation of the deep relationship between God and world, we must be mindful of maintaining the distinct otherness and ultimacy of God. Without radical otherness, God cannot be God; interdependence and mutuality are not possible. The vision of new cosmology that I propose as a lens for viewing reality today is based on the belief that whatever we discover and say about the physical universe, it is God who is ultimately Other and "author of life."[54]

Location affects our way of seeing reality. In my location, the new cosmology is not just an idea; it is steeped in my reality. My husband and I live in a rural farming community by the Ottawa River in eastern Ontario. From our home, we see the marvels and ever-shifting landscape of creation: the earth, sky, and water. The daily drama of the sunrises and sunsets is often heightened by hues of purple, pink, and orange. At times, the night sky seems to be a void, while other nights it is a vault of twinkling diamonds. Deeply influenced by its environment, the river is always changing colour or texture. It can be smooth like a mirror and agitated like the high seas. It seems to flow in a number of directions, depending on the whim of the prevailing winds. Although we try to tame the earth with our domestic seeds and tools, it brings forth its own panoply of wildflowers and berries. I gather with a small community to worship in a white clapboard church. The windows of this modest building were hand-painted long ago with religious symbols and agricultural scenes. There is a strong sense of community when we gather to celebrate and pray for the needs of the people and the land. Before moving here, I lived in the suburbs of Ottawa. From there, I had a very different view of reality. From where I live now, it is easy for me to agree with conviction with O'Murchu's claim that the earth and its surrounding cosmos are alive, and that indeed the universe as a whole is "hospitable to life."[55]

In the new cosmology, the notion of God is also expanded. We move from knowing a transcendent God who intervenes in creation from above to encountering an immanent God who calls forth the dynamic and co-creative dimension of the evolutionary process from within.[56] Attempts to express this new awareness call for a new language to express the co-evolutionary nature of change as well as our changing relationship with God, self, others, and all creation. These efforts are evident in the increasing use of the prefix "co-" in our oral and written communication. Words such as *co-discipleship*[57] came into common usage more than 20 years ago. More recently, *co-presencing*[58] has come to express an even greater depth of attentiveness and relationship. This same language of "co-" has intentionally made its way into the Saint Paul University's ministry formation and pastoral leadership education programs. Students learn to identify themselves as co-learners and co-disciples who are co-responsible for the life and development of their respective communities. As we have seen, language shapes our ways of seeing and being. In learning to speak and act out of this new language, we begin moving toward a more inclusive church.

Feminist thought: An overview

I have invited several companions on this journey into feminist thought, the most notably being Elizabeth Johnson, Letty Russell and Morwenna Griffiths. Like evolutionary thought, feminism offers an alternative way to interpret reality and make sense of life. Although *feminism* is a modern word, the concern to include marginal people, those whom society considered less than human, is not new. Many of the gospel stories show that Jesus' mission of proclaiming and actualizing the reign of God is about transforming the prevailing norms of power and exclusion. Jesus constantly reached out to those who had been excluded by Jewish doctrine or Roman law. His mission was to give flesh to God's unconditional love and abundance by reaching out to lepers, the lame, the blind, children and women, even women whom society considered abject. Jesus' words and actions make it clear for us today: all people are welcome in the reign of God. As theologian Letty Russell says, "Jesus' inclusion of women as disciples, followers, and witnesses stands as a constant correction to the patriarchal biases of religious leaders in his time and in ours."[59]

Feminist thought is consistent with Jesus' concern for inclusion and right use of power. It provides a hermeneutical lens for examining "the ways in which power and control have been exercised at the expense of women, rather than for the liberation of the human community."[60] Women's needs cannot be met without changing our ways of knowing and acting. The feminist way of seeing calls for change that is transformational. This kind of change is not possible without surfacing and critiquing the still predominant patriarchal world view associated with domination and exclusion. In my experience, we are often unaware of the lenses through which we view the world. Patriarchy, which is such a lens, is still very much embedded in our culture.

Feminists are not a monolithic group. They come from a variety of perspectives and do not all view the world from the same place. In the midst of this diversity, feminists uphold one critical principle: the affirmation and promotion of the full humanity of women. This same principle applies to all who are marginalized, be it because of gender, culture, religion, economic status, education, or disability. In feminist theology, there are two main agendas. The first is to raise consciousness of the masculine bias in Christian theology and anthropology, and to analyze how that bias shapes our theological understanding of God, church, ministry, creation, and person. The second is to recover and reconstruct alternative historical traditions and frameworks that support the full personhood of women and their full inclusion in leadership roles. I believe that we can address both these agendas in moving toward a more inclusive church.

Language and change are intrinsically connected to feminist thought. Because language is formative and has a significant socializing function, the reshaping of our God-language cannot be dismissed as a contemporary exercise in political correctness. "Nothing less than the full humanity of women and men and humanity's proper relationship to God" is at stake.[61] Intentionally choosing our religious language can enable change in our religious systems that shape our world view and our Christian identity. Elizabeth Johnson makes this very claim: "Linguistic change and structural change go hand in hand."[62] The regulating bodies of the universal Roman Catholic Church know this point to be true. For example, the new *Roman Missal* (still under review as I write) has restored language that upholds a dualistic theology and anthropology. Although its writers and consultants have been careful to align the English translation with the original Latin text written many centuries ago, they have not taken into account how our view of person and world has changed. For example, when we respond to the presider's greeting "The Lord be with you" by saying "And also with you," we are saying that the human person is a unity of body, mind, and spirit. When, in the new text, we respond, "And also with your spirit," we separate that unity by only focusing on the "divine" element of the person. While that would have been how people would have understood personhood when the Latin text was first written and used, we cannot uncritically retrieve and impose an anthropology that no longer fits our world view.

Another example is the change from "You take away the sin of the world" to "You take away the sins of the world." Again, although this change aligns the English translation with the original Latin, it gives priority to individual sinfulness, to the detriment of bringing before God our "collective guilt or 'sinful structures.'"[63] Although the new missal is being acclaimed by some for its more "dignified language," I stand with those who view it as an attempt to restore and perpetuate dualisms that ensure a clear distinction between church and world, sacred and profane, cleric and lay, individual and community, private and public.

Feminist thought shows us that we all—not only humans but also creation—suffer from the effects of this dualistic world view. It is almost impossible today to extricate feminist thought from its connection to ecology. Listening deeply to the groans of all creation (Romans 8:22), ecofeminism joins together strands of evolutionary and feminist thought as it articulates its concern for mutual empowerment and preservation of the whole universe. An ecofeminist vision of church emphasizes interdependence and the inclusive extension of communion to all "living creatures, ecosystems, and the whole natural world itself."[64] While this vision is about constructing something new, it offers us a new language for expressing our Christian mission of giving life to God's reign in our place and time: "a new earth, a new society and a new religion based on the principle of equal dignity, rights and responsibilities for both women and men, and on the earth principle of the community of all species with their respective dignity, rights and responsibilities."[65] This mission is radically inclusive and challenging. Some may even find it far-fetched. Yet, as we look around us and see the human and ecological destruction caused by violence, greed, and self-righteousness, often in the name of our God and religious practices, we can allow ourselves to wonder whether it is time to imagine other possibilities for realizing our Christian mission.

Language for an alternative world view

I now turn to the five elements drawn from evolutionary and feminist thought that give us language to express a more expansive view of self, other, church, world, creation, and God: energy, consciousness, story, praxis, and system.

1. Energy

In a mechanical view of energy, work and control are the dominant themes. In this view, work effects change in the position, speed, or form of matter. Here, energy has two main forms: it is either potential energy stored for work, or kinetic energy at work. When motion is needed, potential energy is changed into kinetic energy. An example of this is putting gasoline in our car, turning the ignition and moving. Whenever we use energy, it is in its kinetic state. Most of the energy under our control is potential energy, which is produced and distributed as a scarce and depleting resource. Energy is a static resource until we change it from potential to kinetic. That is how we control energy for our use.[66]

The new cosmology expands the static and mechanical notion of energy, viewing energy as a dynamic and mysterious reality with unlimited resourcefulness. In this view, people cannot control energy. Because of its mysterious force, it is usually characterized by movement, instability, and unpredictability. In ancestral religions, the prevailing image of God was that of a spiritually active life force. Today, the Spirit is often likened to the energy at work in all things, including the church. This same link is found in Pope Benedict XVI's first encyclical, *Deus Caritas Est* [God is love], which refers to the Spirit as "also the energy which transforms the heart of the ecclesial community."[67]

In the new cosmology, energy plays a central role in the life of the universe. The new cosmology sees all existence as imbued with three energies. The language used to describe these three energies expresses a three-movement change process, which gives shape and direction to all being and becoming. The first energy is *differentiation*. As the name suggests, differentiation is the power to be different. Parents of adolescents have seen the power of differentiation, even though we may have never used this language. I learned what that power meant when my daughter was 14. I asked her why she no longer looked forward to spending weekends with us on the boat. She used to enjoy those times together. My daughter replied, "That was before I had a life." She was telling me that our life as a family and her life as a teenage girl were no longer the same. She was changing, moving from what we could call her parents' external control or outer authority to greater autonomy. Differentiation is the first step of the change process. On its own, differentiation is potentially dangerous, since it is more concerned with innovation and renewal than self-preservation.

The second energy is *autopoiesis*. In Greek, *poiesis* means to "make" or "create." Evolutionary thought uses the words *auto* and *poiesis* to show that all life forms have the power within to remake themselves.

Autopoiesis is the power within to self-organize, self-renew, and self-transcend in ways that are consistent with our histories.[68] Contrary to differentiation's concern with novelty and difference, autopoiesis guides the process of change such that it maintains the integrity of our fundamental identity or mission. When my teenage daughter started moving toward greater independence, she was still my daughter, although at times she spoke differently and had different priorities than previously. Yet she was still being guided by her own identity and fundamental values. That reality became more apparent after rather than during this stage of the change process. In adult education, we often use the phrase *trust the process*. It captures the essence of this stage of the change process. We can all experience differentiation and *autopoiesis* as chaotic and involving a loss of meaning. This is often when we try to restore what seemed like the "golden years." Paradoxically, it is often our need to maintain ourselves that leads us to change.

The third energy in the three-part movement is communion, which comes from the Latin for "mutual participation." Communion is the power to draw all of creation into mutual interdependence. In the new cosmology, relationship is the nature and goal of all existence. "Experiences of communion make us keenly aware that we are bound to others by something that transcends, grounds and enlivens us, but that we do not control," says Patricia O'Connell Killen.[69] Communion is the destiny of all beings.

Evolutionary thought stretches our understanding of energy and communion even further with the theory of holons, a scientific theory that has evolved from the ongoing search for the ultimate in reality. Not long ago, we believed that all of reality was composed of atoms. In an atomistic view of reality, we only see individuals. Societies are simply a collection of individuals, "a collection that has no independent reality whatsoever."[70] When we use the language of the "sins of the world," we uphold this atomistic view. As science progressed through the twentieth century, the theory of atoms gave way to the notion that subatomic particles and waves are the ultimate reality. More recently, a quantum view of reality has expanded that view into the theory of holons, which claims that all of "reality is composed not of things nor processes nor wholes nor parts, but of whole/parts, of holons."[71] Every whole is a part and every part is a whole. Whatever exists in the universe is a whole/part, in which individuality and communion co-exist. In this view of reality, rather than desiring to isolate any dimension of reality in order to explain its unique individuality, we seek out the larger whole to which it belongs and explore its uniqueness in terms of its relationship within the greater whole. As a whole/part, I am an I/we, a unique individual member in a "social system that is a dimension of my own being-in-the-world."[72] As an individual holon, I am an I/we who perceives reality from both my unique perspective and from the perspective of the whole of which I am a part, a whole that is part of a larger whole. Each part affects and is affected by the whole. Each whole affects and is affected by its parts.

The theory of holons gives us a language to express the reality of discipleship and church today, including the story of the Centre for Ministry Formation at Saint Paul University. Through this lens, we cannot explain the uniqueness of an individual disciple or of an individual centre for ministry formation without looking at its relationship to the greater whole of the mission of the Risen Christ enfleshed in the church. What the Centre is and does is affected by its individual members as well as the whole church. Each member as well as the church as a whole is affected by what the Centre is and does. Through the concept of whole/parts, we cannot make meaning of the church's mission without taking into consideration its relationship to all of creation as part of the socio-historical context in which we live as disciples. Each dimension of this reality is part of an interactive system in which nothing remains static or stable.

Our conventional mode of reasoning—linear thinking—makes the whole/parts concept somewhat difficult to hold together. We usually define reality as being either a whole or a part, not both. This idea of whole/parts challenges our modern tendency for compartmentalization and fragmentation—a tendency that affects our anthropological, cosmological, theological, and ecclesiological doctrines. This evolutionary concept of energy and holons offers us an alternative way to view reality, with interconnectedness and interdependence being its defining marks. As I have grappled with finding a way to make sense of the many facets of a change process, I found this theory helpful for seeing reality as a complex web in which both individual parts and the whole are consistently affected and bound together by the energy of communion. Each of the following concepts offers us opportunities to see how energy is at the core of reality.

2. *Consciousness*

A conventional definition of *consciousness* describes it as awareness of ourselves as well as of our surroundings. An evolutionary view of consciousness goes beyond the human qualities of awareness to seeing us as being deeply interconnected with the consciousness of the universe. Humans participate in the unfolding of the universal consciousness by bringing to "conscious awareness the consciousness out of which our own self-awareness is born."[73] In this deep interconnectedness, the inner wisdom and intelligence of evolution reveal a world of greater complexity, openness, fluidity, and creativity than we might otherwise see.[74] Consciousness is present within universal life as an ongoing series of self-organizing processes that become more and more complex. All of reality has the potential for transformation to a higher order of consciousness and complexity.

In an evolutionary view of the world as growing in universal consciousness, we can see behaviour with new eyes. This new way of seeing has an immense influence on our self-awareness as well as on our image of God. We move from stressing the more traditional Darwinian concerns of scarcity, randomness, and competition to emphasizing abundance, co-creativity, and cooperation."[75] Relying on predictable outcomes through cause-and-effect explanations gives way to discovering patterns, rhythms, and relationships that begin to make sense. In this view, we move from subject-object relations, in which we attribute greater agency to certain people to act upon others as passive objects, toward inter-subjective relations that give space to co-create new actions together.[76]

The nineteenth century was a fertile time for developing human consciousness. One notable thinker of that era was the German philosopher Georg Hegel, who continues to challenge our still conventional tendency to favour a world view that is causal, atomistic, and instrumentalist. In his many writings, and particularly in his *Philosophy of History and Action*, Hegel proposes a developmental, process-oriented perception of reality that transcends the dualism of individual (I) and community (we) as well as the divide between the outer event (how we act) and the inner state (how we think and feel).[77] Marked by this type of anti-dualist view of reality, the emergence of historical consciousness enables us to enter into the dynamic of historical transformation, which makes it possible for us to become subjects—intentional moral agents—rather than victims or "pawns of history."[78] Historical consciousness has opened up new perspectives on our Jesus story as well as on the practices of the early Christian communities.[79] When we are able to see our concerns and issues in the larger socio-historical context, and "recognize the complex relationships and structures that shape individuals and societies,"[80] we have a greater capacity to "walk upright" as we grow into fullness of life.

In the early nineteenth century, a specifically feminist consciousness also began to rise. Sarah Grimké, an American feminist activist, theorist and abolitionist, remains a powerful influence on the rise of feminist consciousness today.[81] Until then, women's experience had always been nearly invisible; when noticed, it was included as part of men's experience. There was little awareness that women's experience *as* woman's experience was relevant to intellectual work. With the rise of consciousness of women as women, specifically in a Christian context, the Bible became a basis for arguing either for or against women's rights and injustices. This growing self-awareness marked the beginning of women's movement toward self-empowerment, of acquiring greater control over their own lives as subjects of their own actions and as authors of the meaning of their own stories. As the feminist consciousness unfolds, autopoietic energy gives shape and direction to the process of renewal and reconstruction.

For feminists, consciousness opens the way to discernment and action. The feminist movement has witnessed and continues to witness to the call to action for social change. Women's consciousness-raising groups provide optimum opportunities for personal and social transformation by telling and reflecting on women's stories. Language is a key issue in feminist consciousness; it shapes our identities and can enable or disable change toward greater inclusivity and inter-subjectivity.

3. Story

Language and story are at the heart of feminist thought. Story anchors our lives in the contexts in which we live and is vital to our search for meaning and truth in our lives and in the lives of others. As we tell and reflect upon stories in community, we become more self-aware and contribute to a developing consciousness that is greater than our own. In that movement, the energy of differentiation bids us to claim the uniqueness of our story and keeps us from collapsing into uniformity and homogeneity. Without the concreteness of our story, we remain disembodied and faceless in a mass of anonymity. Until the rise of feminist consciousness, women's stories were not spoken; there was no space for those stories to be heard. As a result, women remained faceless with respect to men. They were not recognized in the fullness of their dignity as human beings; hence, women were denied the rights and responsibilities ascribed to those who were regarded as fully human. Feminist theologian Mary Malone has contributed much to our growing consciousness in this regard by collecting and publishing the stories of many medieval Christian women.[82]

As we view reality through a feminist lens, we see that beginning with personal experience is crucial to the process of renewal and reconstruction. However, telling that story is only one component in the search for meaning. Each story must be received, honoured for its own dignity, and treated critically through reflection and rethinking. Truth is encountered and meaning is constructed in the continuous back and forth between experience and reflection. This process of reflecting and rethinking must necessarily include attention to political perspectives, power, and, of course, language.[83] Furthermore, this feminist process of reflection, rethinking, and theorizing cannot be a solitary activity. This is a dialogical process with others in community, in a spirit of openness to critique from other viewpoints and perspectives.[84] When we embrace this spirit of openness, we risk discovering new information and changing our ways of seeing.

Feminist theory has helped sharpen my own attention to the power of language to determine what we know, how we know, and what we do because of what we know. In 2001, the North American Friends of Sabeel, a justice and peace project of Palestinian Christians living in the Holy Land, produced a film that aims to raise awareness of the conflict in the Middle East. As the group's website indicates, it is its hope that viewers of the film "will be inspired to become active in striving for justice and peace for the region."[85] The film's title, *Stuck with the Truth*, acknowledges that once we know a different truth, we cannot simply go back to what we knew before. Change in what we know can inspire us to action. A feminist view of change calls us to bear responsibility for some kind of action aimed at individual and social change.

4. Praxis

The concept of praxis is related to the concepts of consciousness and story. Praxis consists of attention, reflection, and change that is future-oriented and liberating. To illustrate how this concept gives us a more inclusive and dynamic view of reality, it is helpful to compare and contrast the terms *praxis* and *practice*. Both mean action that aims to achieve a particular end or goal. The action taken is never value-free, nor is it without meaning. This is where the similarity ends. Praxis involves attention, reflection and change; practice does not. When it comes to practice, we do not pay attention to the beliefs and values that pervade our actions. The difference between praxis and practice, therefore, is found in Socratic wisdom: "An unexamined life is not worth living."

In practice, our attention is focused only on the goals of our action, not on the means we take to achieve those goals. If we do not attend to the values and beliefs inherent in our actions, as well as to the means and goals of our actions, our actions remain unreflective and superficial. We are unaffected by the action itself. Without reflective or intentional action, we are not moved to change, to think or act differently. Unreflective actions perpetuate more unreflective actions, creating a cyclical pattern in which there is no possibility for change. A familiar way of expressing this phenomenon is "going in a vicious circle" or "chasing our tails." An unreflected life remains static; it is denied the possibility of further growth.

Praxis, on the other hand, is reflective; for that reason, it is action that is both value directed and theory laden. In praxis, we attend to both the means and the goal of our action in order to assess their validity in light of the vision that guides the action to achieving its goal. In praxis, reflection and action occur simultaneously. Because praxis is intentionally reflective action, we attend to the meaning *within* our actions. We notice the values and operative theories in our actions; we think about them and critically reflect on them in light of our professed theories.[86]

What we do as Christians, both individually and collectively, matters. As my story and the story of the Centre for Ministry Formation at Saint Paul University show, the meaning of what we do sometimes contradicts what we profess to be the beliefs and values to which we are committed. In praxis, we can get in touch with that incongruence.

That is the first step. We can then put that experience in dialogue with alternative theories to broaden and deepen our understanding of the truth that our praxis has revealed. Praxis is always future-oriented, yet it is not to be equated with or limited to physical action. Critical reflection can be in itself change-oriented and liberating, particularly since it catalyzes a deeper consciousness of and change in our ways of knowing. This change eventually leads to responsible action.

Feminist theory is embedded in the praxis of justice and advocacy for the poor and oppressed, especially women. Here we discover a yearning for a world in which the dignity of all creation, and the equal rights and responsibilities of both men and women, are the norm. This is the vision of the fullness of life in which all of creation is called to freely participate. For feminists, praxis can be authentic or inauthentic. Anything that denies or diminishes the full humanity of women is deemed inauthentic. For feminist theologians, inauthentic praxis does not reflect divine revelation, authentic relation to the divine or authentic faith community. Inauthentic social and inauthentic ecclesial praxis hides the truth of God's being: the truth of God's being-for-us and the truth of our-being-for-each-other.[87] Authentic praxis promotes the full humanity of women and men as well as the dignity of all creation. The narrative process of story and reflection is praxis—the back-and-forth movement between experience and theory that embodies attention, consciousness, and action oriented toward greater freedom. We begin our journey into freedom in the praxis of telling our stories, reflecting on them, rethinking them in community, and opening ourselves to alternative frames of reference.

5. System

A conventional understanding of *system* is that it is an orderly, interconnected, and complex arrangement of parts or units. Systems can be material and visibly concrete, and include such things as our physical bodies and institutions. Theories are also visible systems. As a human institution, the church is a visibly concrete system. Over time, the church has developed a "systematic theology," an ordered system of theories about God, humans, church, and world. Systems can also be invisible—that is, hidden from our own consciousness. For instance, our mental structures are invisible systems that order the way we make meaning of reality. We are often not aware of our meaning systems and the assumptions we carry, yet they have a powerful hold on determining what is real and true for us. Faith has a significant influence on our meaning systems and our actions that flow from them. Our Scripture tradition witnesses to people who have acted on faith as their meaning systems. Faith enables us to see and know what is real for us, even though that reality remains concretely invisible (Hebrews 11:1). For instance, Abraham and Sarah left their homeland on faith. The biblical stories of the Annunciation and the Visitation also witness to this reality.

Through the lens of new science, *all* of life takes the form of systems that are constantly undergoing change. The new science makes a distinction between open and closed systems. I have found this distinction very helpful for understanding the underlying structures for change and non-change. Closed and open systems have something very important in common: both are ingeniously designed for self-preservation. Closed systems seek to preserve themselves by maintaining equilibrium and stability. Open systems do so by intentionally keeping themselves in disequilibrium or off balance. These distinct ways of ensuring self-preservation help us see why some individuals and organizations are more immune to change than others.

Closed systems give priority to maintaining their structure by using energy to insulate themselves from whatever might deviate them from their original course. However, contrary to popular belief, equilibrium is not a positive state but rather the "end state in the evolution of a closed system."[88] As the name suggests, closed systems actually close themselves to renewal by cutting themselves off from usable energy that is available inside or outside of itself. Without usable energy, closed systems eventually deteriorate or die. Open systems use energy very differently. They exchange their used energy for usable energy in their environment. Open systems use energy for novelty and renewal in order to stay viable over time.

In a systems view of reality, energy is equated with feedback. All systems produce feedback that is looped back into the system so it can make whatever adjustments it needs to preserve itself. Our human biological immune system is a good example of feedback loops; this is our way of dealing with infections or viruses. Feedback loops are available in the systems' internal *and* external environments. Open and closed systems seek out and use feedback very differently; yet, both are intent on self-preservation. Closed systems control the feedback loops and interpret the information to regulate or defend against change. For closed systems, feedback is negative, since it signals a divergence from predetermined goals. Open systems have an open relationship to feedback. They use feedback to notice something new and positive, which it then amplifies in order to destabilize itself. Positive feedback is essential to the ability to adapt and change.

Unfortunately, open systems are usually associated with chaos, and our fear of chaos usually moves us to rush in and attempt to stabilize that which is out of order. Paradoxically, when faced with increasing levels of disturbances, open systems have the innate ability to self-organize to deal with new information. The self-organizing system's "stability comes from a deepening center, a clarity about who it is, what it needs and what is required to survive in its environment."[89] In its bid to maintain and produce itself, "the system chooses a path into the future that it believes is congruent with who is it has been."[90] "This is autopoiesis in action."[91] Open systems trust in the power of autopoietic energy.

Rather than fearfully reacting to their environment, open systems work in partnership with it. This calls for a new way of understanding freedom, boundaries, and autonomy. A clear sense of identity is crucial for achieving autonomy from the environment, giving it greater freedom to decide how it will respond. Boundaries are not defined externally for the system, but rather, "the boundary lives *within the system*,"[92] becoming visible as the system explores its space of possibilities. Boundaries "not only create distinctions; they are also places for communication and exchange."[93] Over time, openness to the environment makes for stronger systems that are less susceptible to externally induced changes.

The viability of self-organizing systems comes from their capacity to create structures that fit the current reality. However, when we deify systems, we protect their structures in order to maintain their identity. An evolutionary view of reality shows us that systems are not simply defined by their form or function. Rather, they are process structures that reorganize into different forms to maintain their identity. The system may maintain itself in its present form or it may evolve into a new form, depending on what is required. No living system is locked into one structure; it is capable of organizing into whatever form it determines best suits the current situation.[94]

Conclusion

Evolutionary and feminist thought offer us new ways of seeing reality. When we incorporate energy, consciousness, story, praxis, and system into a more expansive world view, we may find ourselves attending to, welcoming, and perhaps honouring even more the dynamic nature of all of life. When we truly believe that communion is God's desire for all creation, then energy becomes a force to be embraced even when we might lack the courage or trust in the Spirit's immanent wisdom to keep us faithful to our essential mission and identity as Jesus' disciples. In the back and forth between story and reflection, I have come to see how my own story as well as my family story is closely linked with the developing story of ministry formation at Saint Paul University. What was, at one time, a latent anger and unconscious desire for greater inclusivity has developed into a clearer sense of call to risk working to transform inauthentic practices and structures. That call is not only personal, but also transcends my own little story and sits in a much broader socio-historical context that holds together the past, present, and future of both church and world. In paying attention to and reflecting upon my own educational praxis, I have become clearer about the intrinsic link between what I do and what I think and feel. It is only in examining and critiquing the values, biases, theories, and world views that shape my behaviours and praxis that I can change my way of being with and for others.

A systems view of reality can open the way for understanding much of the immunity to change that arises in attempts to move toward a more inclusive church. Institutions in general tend to be closed systems, giving priority to tradition rather than novelty. The church is no exception. When we understand the current Roman Catholic Church structure to be divinely ordered, we make every effort to maintain the status quo, to stave off change. However, the Second Vatican Council is very clear in its call to "read the signs of the times." This proposition can be considered rather risky, especially when we couple it with an understanding of our church structure as more of an open than closed system. Here, our concern for self-preservation no longer holds us captive to repeating our history and protecting ourselves from change. Rather, the desire for self-preservation can free us to pay attention to the feedback—to "read the signs of the times"—in our internal and external environments. A view of reality through the lens of self-organizing systems can help us transcend some of the linear thinking and dualisms that keep us from moving toward a more inclusive church. From this view, we hold in tension many paradoxes—form and process, being and becoming, autonomy and belonging, stasis and dynamism, freedom and order—each of which is inherent to all life forms.

No individual or organization is a fully open or fully closed system. We all live lives filled with paradox. For individuals, there are times when we tend to be more open than closed or vice versa. All of us "experience an inherent tension between stability and openness."[95] The elements I have shared from my own story witness to this truth. I now see more clearly the time I was much more closed to feedback and used a lot of energy maintaining control over my own family and immediate environment. I now see that "anger is a vital passion filled with energy."[96] Anger was the feedback I could no longer ignore. It was giving me "vital information about the quality of my connections to self, others, God and earth."[97] I have come to realize that ignoring its messages seriously hampered my capacity to live and love more fully. When I reflect on that time of my life, I lament all the energy I wasted trying to deny my anger and maintain a perfect family. That was toxic for me—physically, psychologically, and spiritually.

Years ago, when I was considering studying theology, I mentioned to a member of my local parish that I was planning to attend Saint Paul University. She quickly answered, "Don't go there. You will lose your faith." As I reflect on her reaction through this chapter's lens of evolutionary and feminist thinking, I see that she wanted to keep me from being exposed to new information that she believed would keep me from living as a committed Christian. I can say that I was intentionally looking for new information that would help me grow in faith. My parish community could no longer answer the questions I had about living my faith, and I was feeling a need to differentiate myself from my immediate parish community. Well, I did go to Saint Paul University and I did not lose my faith. In fact, my identity and mission as a disciple of the Risen Christ have become even stronger. What I lost was the narrow structure or form in which I had practised my faith. That structure has expanded to include a range of ways of celebrating and developing my faith. It has become clear to me that when we cling to and identify with a single temporal form or structure, we cut ourselves off from the dynamic process that fosters life.

Not everyone is for change. Often change brings conflict and resistance. We no longer fit the same way we used to into our relationships and communities. This has certainly been my experience. Some people in my community reacted negatively when I began to expand my ways of seeing how God was active in my life, in the life of the church, and in the world. For example, one person sent me an article entitled "A Sacrament Is Not a Rainbow," which drew a very clear line between God's self-revelation in the world and God's self-revelation in the church. While I appreciated her concern that my orthodoxy not become waylaid by spiritual fads, I have come to recognize that in trying to stop people from exploring new points of view, we immunize ourselves and others from change that is constructive and life-giving.

4

God-language and God Image: Retrieving a God of Relationship

What we say about God affects who we are and what we do. Conversely, what we say and do affects our image of God. Whether or not we are conscious of this fact, there is a deep connection between our God-language and our social-political reality. Our vision of God, world, and church is inextricably interconnected with our praxis. Our God-language not only shapes our praxis but it also stands as a profound critique of what we do to live out our mission.[98] This same truth inspired the Second Vatican Council's call to retrieve the Trinitarian image of God as the "starting point, context, and goal of all theological reflection and practical planning for matters internal and external to ecclesial life."[99] If returning to Trinitarian theology is to enable us to make meaning for our Christian vocation today, then that retrieval must also address the question of our God-language as it relates to the concerns of our time.

I have come to appreciate the existential power of the triune symbol of God in my own life as well as in my context of ministry. Our God-image has a powerful influence on how we choose and act. I believe that rediscovering and gaining a deeper understanding of certain aspects of that symbol can inspire authentic ecclesial praxis. When humans engage in authentic praxis in a critical, conscious way, we pursue our vocation of becoming more fully human. In authentic praxis, relationality, interdependence, and connectedness define the core around which Christian life and practice are to be interpreted and understood.

The language I have chosen to retrieve the triune symbol promotes the full humanity of women, men, and children, values all creation, and points to the dynamic and inclusive nature of the church.

Evolutionary and feminist thought show us that we all belong to a story that continues to unfold. Story has been and continues to be pivotal to the human search for meaning, a search that is intrinsically related to our ways of knowing and understanding truth. Story has the power to move us beyond our conventional horizons for viewing and defining reality. Our Christian story, told and retold throughout the ages, is the story of our experience of encounter with holy mystery. All Christian doctrine flows from that story in the back-and-forth movement between experience and reflection. As this chapter demonstrates, the language we use to tell our story of encounter with the triune God matters. The retrieval and interpretation of some of the ancient language for God offers us opportunities to expand our imagination, giving us fresh ways of seeing God and creation.

Retrieving the Trinitarian symbol

According to Catherine Mowry LaCugna, any critical retrieval of Trinitarian theology must be situated within the Christian story of salvation, which holds together inquiries into "God's life with us and our life with each other."[100] There is but one life of the triune God, a life in which we have been graciously included as partners. In other words, we cannot separate God's being from God's being-for-us; nor can we separate God's being and God's being-for-us from our being-for-each-other.[101] God is in communion with humanity in the reality of salvation history. Therefore, our Trinitarian doctrine is "ultimately a practical doctrine with radical consequences for Christian life."[102]

Some Christians use the term *treasure chest* to describe our doctrinal tradition, implying that we protect and pass on our heritage intact from one generation of believers to the next. Yet a historical review of Trinitarian doctrine shows that doctrines are not self-enclosed boxes or static truths that capture our experience of God's salvific presence and action in our lives. Through the lens of open and closed systems, we can see that our tradition has developed and continues to evolve in response to the concerns of a particular time. When the concerns change, we return to our tradition with new questions. Those questions are the feedback that could signal a call for change. When we blind ourselves to feedback that indicates that we need to take another look at what was right and good for another time and place, we cut ourselves off from the opportunity to discern fresh ways for living our mission today. When our main concern is defending ourselves against the forces of change, our doctrines can fossilize and become relics of a distant past with little relevance to life today. On the other hand, when we allow our living traditions to engage with current realities, they are freed from "debilitating accretions"[103] and a creative energy is released. As systems theory shows, this paradox is life-giving. The creative energy that moves us to change keeps us faithful to our fundamental mission of revealing the liberating God who is encountered in history.

Like all doctrine, Trinitarian doctrine is a unified system of beliefs that have gone through a series of controversies and formulations. A historical review of this doctrine shows that it is not a closed system, especially in the first five centuries of Christianity. The practices and feedback in that socio-historical environment had immense influence in establishing our Trinitarian formula. The best known of those formulas is the Nicene Creed, which dates back to the Council of Nicea in 325 CE. Each formulation came about in a particular context, in dialogue with the concerns and issues of the time. At the Council of Nicea, as well as the Council of Chalcedon in the fifth century, Western and Eastern pastoral leaders were concerned with safeguarding the at once divinity and humanity of Jesus Christ. Their main preoccupation was to present a theory that would stave off the controversies that either denied or diminished both the divine and human nature of Jesus Christ.[104] The leaders' concern with how the theory would affect the ordering and practice of Christian life co-determined their final version of the Trinitarian doctrine. And although the Chalcedonian doctrine of the Trinity incorporated the already rich Trinitarian heritage that had developed in the years and even centuries prior to that Council, it was systematized according to the philosophical, anthropological, cultural, scientific, and religious thinking of the fifth century. The Platonic doctrine of universals shaped the prevailing world view in which early Greek theologians "drew a parallel between the Christian doctrine of the unity of God" and the philosophical theory of "one God-head."[105] Our world view has changed since the fifth century. Questions that emerge from our current ecclesial praxis guide the retrieval of our Trinitarian symbol today: How do we live our Christian vocation as disciples today? How does our Trinitarian doctrine inspire our response to participate in the Risen Christ's mission of humanization and transformation of *this* world?

Feminist consciousness has revealed the power of the symbols and language we use in our search for meaning. Intentionally shaping our religious language, particularly our God-language, is an integral element of ecclesial and social praxis. Feminists have raised our awareness of the exclusive male imagery that has been used for the triune God for nearly 2,000 years. They argue that as long as God is addressed only in masculine language, God will be conceived as male. And if God is seen and worshipped only as male, then human males will appear to be more like God than females are. Since so many Christians have come to these same conclusions, we cannot responsibly deny the connection between language and practice.[106]

My own experience has shown this conclusion to be true. A few years ago, I overheard a conversation between two men discussing their relationships with their children. One said, "I often look to God as the source of my own fatherhood. This gives me much strength and consolation in my way of being with my children." The other affirmed that this was also his experience. These two men have been well-formed in our liturgical tradition, as this same image of God as "the source and origin of all fatherhood" is part of the official prayer of the church.[107] And yet, it leaves us with many questions: If our God-image is so important to our image as human beings, what happens when that image is exclusive to men alone? If God is the source of fatherhood, who is the source of motherhood? Is that source any less than divine? While a father image rightly makes us radically dependent on God's mercy, compassion, and grace, it is not enough. If "Father" is the prevailing God-language that shapes our identity and practice as disciples, we stymie our call to live the paradox of being simultaneously dependent, independent, and interdependent disciples in our relationships with God, self, and the world. Change in our image of God will remain superficial unless we address the assumptions that underlie our current patriarchal and androcentric symbol. Reshaping our God-language is difficult and serious. Although we could be tempted to dismiss it as a contemporary exercise in political correctness, what is involved, as feminists have shown us, is "nothing less than the full humanity of women and men and humanity's proper relationship to God."[108]

When we attend to the concerns and issues of our times, we notice a recurring theme of relationships. What are right relationships today—with ourselves, with others, with the earth, with God? This question of right relationships emerges from both our personal and collective lives. In putting this question in dialogue with our tradition, I draw on two ancient concepts—*perichoresis* and *koinonia*—both of which recapture, reconnect, reconstruct, and rediscover the power and richness of Trinitarian theology. These two concepts are the basis for understanding Trinitarian doctrine as a theology of relationship. Reformist feminist theology and Eastern Orthodox tradition offer ways to retrieve and reconstruct a Trinitarian theology of relationship that speaks to our nature and mission of moving toward a more inclusive church. For LaCugna, a Trinitarian theology of relationship "explores the mysteries of love, relationship, personhood and communion, within the framework of God's self-revelation in the person of Christ and the activity of the Spirit."[109] For Eastern Orthodox theologian John Zizioulas, a Trinitarian theology of relationship stands at the core of personal and ecclesial being: God's being and human beings are essentially marked by "Being as Communion."[110] To exist is to be in communion with one other.

I began this chapter by claiming that there is a deep connection between our God-language and our social-political reality. Many would argue that Trinitarian doctrine has very little effect on our lives as Christians. This argument is not surprising; the concept of the triune God is not easy to get our minds around. Yet whether or not we are aware of it or reflect on it, this concept does have a significant effect on our personal and collective lives as Christians. This influence is evident in our ways of being in relationship with one another and in the hierarchic ordering of our ministries and ecclesial praxis. This is just as true for us today as it was in the earliest days of the church.

Revisiting the source for Eastern and Western Trinitarian doctrines

In the fifth century, the Council of Chalcedon claimed in Christ what it called a *hypostatic* union of two natures—divine and human—without confusion, without change, without division, without separation. Like the contemporary theory of holons, the ancient concept of hypostatic union challenges our conventional mode of linear thinking for making sense of reality. Some argue that a leap of faith is needed to believe that Jesus is both divine and human. The Greek term *hypostasis,* or what we call *hypostatic union* in English, refers to communion. For the Greek theologians from the region of Cappadocia[111] *hypostasis* was the measuring stick for judging authentic Christian praxis. However, before we too quickly determine that communion is the norm by which all Christian praxis is deemed authentic or inauthentic, it would be useful to revisit the statement made in the previous chapter that there is an intrinsic connection between our religious consciousness and our world view, which shapes what we know to be real and true. Given this claim, we can ask this question: What is the relationship between the fifth-century Greek world view and the religious consciousness of that time? In other words, what is the mode of being-in-the-world referred to in the fifth-century text that we refer to as the Definition of the Faith?[112] To answer that question, we must do a critical retrieval of the Chalcedonian theological, anthropological, and ecclesiological understanding of person (*prosopon*) and substance (*ousia*) in comparison to the predominant Western paradigm for personhood.[113] While this brief review is rather technical, it does reveal a major point for identifying how conventional Western Trinitarian thinking has come to perpetuate attitudes of domination and control in its communion theologies.

The key to understanding this Western tendency is found in the distinction between the Western and Eastern understanding of *hypostasis*. The West identified *hypostasis* with substance (*ousia*), whereas the East associated it with personhood (*prosopon*). It seems that the Greek philosophers of the time understood personhood as an open and dynamic reality that exists only in reference to others. In other words, personhood could only be actualized in communion. This Greek view of personhood became the framework for the Chalcedonian Trinitarian formula, in which the being of God is identified first and foremost with *prosopon*. In this system, it is God's personal existence that forms God's substance, or *ousia*. Furthermore, because the essence of God is personhood, there is no divine substance, no God, outside the Trinity.[114]

Given the diversity of thought and context in which the Trinitarian controversies have taken place, no church council has unanimously agreed on the final formulation and interpretation of doctrine. While the text of the Chalcedonian formula continues to be fundamental to the Christological development throughout the Latin West and much of the East, there is ongoing disagreement on the interpretation of that formula, particularly with respect to *hypostasis, prosopon* and *ousia.* The Latin West continues to associate *hypostasis* with a more conventional atomistic concept of person as centre or individual consciousness, particularly as that concept relates to the ontological categories assigned to both God and humanity. This Western interpretation of person in our Trinitarian doctrine has significant influence on our ecclesial and social praxis.

The Eastern understanding of person gives primacy to the concept of person as a relational being, breaking down the isolation and solitariness of both the human and divine, all the while respecting the radical otherness of the other. In this view, relationality neither constrains the freedom nor diminishes the uniqueness of the person. Rather, it is in self-transcendence, in the movement beyond the limits of our own selves toward the other, that we actualize ourselves as unique and unrepeatable persons made in the image of God. A retrieval of this Eastern view of person has significant implications for our image of God, our own self-understanding as human persons made in the image of God, and for our Christian life and practice. In this view of Trinitarian theology, baptism is regarded as new birth into a network of relationships that transcends exclusiveness, and "salvation is not a matter of moral perfection [or] an improvement of nature, but a new hypostasis of nature, a new creation."[115]

Our ecclesial praxis is also very much influenced by the difference with which Eastern and Western theologies address the issue of the procession of the Holy Spirit in their respective Trinitarian doctrines. For the East, the Holy Spirit proceeds from the Father, whereas in the Western *filioque* doctrine,[116] the Holy Spirit proceeds from both Father and the Son. Although the source of the latter is the Latin form of the Creed from 381 CE, it was introduced into the Nicene Creed after 1014 on papal authority alone.[117] This doctrine has never been accepted in the Christian East, which maintains that the Spirit proceeds only from the Father. Although Eastern Trinitarian theology preserves the monarchic identity of the Father who begets both Son and Spirit, it also maintains that the three persons of the Trinity are radically equal, yet different from each other. The West tends to locate difference in substance (*ousia*), whereas the East situates difference in the ways each of the three persons (*prosopon*) relates to the others. In contrast to the Western emphasis on the unity of the divine essence and substance, Eastern Trinitarian theology emphasizes that in the divine life is found an energetic relationship of interdependence and mutuality among the three persons, including the Spirit and the Son. The three persons are distinct in their relation to each other. For the East, "person" is first and foremost relational; therefore, the unity of God lives in the person, not in the substance of God.[118]

While the technicality of this doctrine can overshadow its relevance to our concerns today, the difference between the Eastern and Western doctrines has an effect on our theology and practice. The Eastern structure of ecclesial authority reflects its Trinitarian doctrine by placing collegiality at the heart of decision making. The Western *filioque* upholds a hierarchical doctrine that gives priority to the unity of substance in the Father-Son relationship at the expense of the full deity of the Spirit. The result is the emphasis on the separateness and individuality of each divine person to the detriment of their interrelatedness and interdependence.[119] Although some may have never heard of the *filioque* doctrine by name, when we reflect on our ecclesial praxis or pastoral leadership education programs, we can see it informing the values and theories found there. In our traditional Roman Catholic theology of ministry, the priest is configured to Christ, isolating ministry from the community. This same theology underlies the separation between church and world, especially in its structures of power and authority.

Unless we go back to the source of our tradition with our current issues and questions, we risk creating more disconnection between the various ministries that are emerging today. No theory or theology can fully explain the mysteries of our faith. However, Eastern theology can expand our Western understanding of aspects of our Trinitarian doctrine, particularly in its view of person and relationship among the persons of the Trinity. The Eastern emphasis on relationship can help move us from giving priority to isolation and independence toward relations of interdependence and mutuality that honour the tension between autonomy and inclusion in our journey into wholeness.

In classical Western theology, the *filioque* doctrine associates the solitary God with a static and monolithic unity of divine nature. Here, God is protected from the "perceived threat of plurality."[120] However, a critical retrieval of our Trinitarian theology allows us to see in our triune symbol "differentiated unity of variety or manifoldness, in which there is distinction, inner richness and complexity." Our Greek origins give us a language to envision this unity-in-diversity with the terms *perichoresis* and *koinonia*.

Perichoresis

The theological term *perichoresis* comes from the Greek word *perichoreo,* which was commonly used in seventh-century Greek culture to signify "cyclical movement or recurrence."[121] Although many of us do not use this Greek term, Western Christians may be familiar with the phrase *mutual indwelling* to describe *perichoretic* relations. *Perichoresis* may be interpreted in two ways. It may mean either simply dwelling or resting in the other, giving it a more static meaning, or it may indicate a more "dynamically interweaving of things with each other."[122] The Western church has opted for the more static interpretation, equating it with the Latin translation of the term, which means "sitting and seat."[123] The Eastern church has tended to use the more dynamic interpretation, which expresses the "dynamic and vital character of each divine person, as well as the coinherence and immanence of each divine person in the other two."[124] The Eastern understanding of *perichoresis* as "being-in-one-another, permeation without confusion"[125] holds together both individuality and community. This view of *perichoresis* provides a dynamic model of persons in communion—a model based on mutuality, interdependence, and inter-subjectivity—as it locates unity in diversity, in a true communion of persons in relation with one another. This doctrine claims that "each of the divine persons interpenetrates and dwells in the other two."[126] *Perichoresis* is not simply an idea of the inner relations of the triune God. With eyes and hearts of faith, Christians experience it as the self-communication of God's being. It expresses our life in God, God's being for us, as well as our being for each other. Our ecclesial praxis does not simply imitate or reflect God's immanent characteristics of mutuality of the indwellingness, it is literally shaped and informed by the actual experience of the "mutual indwelling and encircling of God's holy mystery"[127] in the very fabric of our lives.

As first articulated in the Chalcedonian formula, Jesus is the *hypostasis*—the communion of divine and human. In Jesus the divine and the human are one, "without separation, without mingling, without confusion."[128] Jesus is both who and what God is: "infinite capacity for communion."[129] Jesus is also "who and what we are to become."[130] Discipleship is a way of life in which we continually seek to respond to God's call to be fully human. As disciples, we continuously seek, through the power of the Spirit, to enter more deeply into relationship with the person of Jesus Christ. Jesus is what our own humanity was created to be: "theonomous, catholic, and in communion, in right relationship, with every creature and with God."[131] It is in the dance of the Trinity, the communion of persons, that we find the source and reference for being a truly theonomous self, "a self patterned in relatedness to a relational God for the sake of the world."[132] Rooted in a relational God, our call to catholicity is a call to inclusivity, to celebrate and partner in God's all-embracing communion.

Although the doctrine of *perichoresis* is fully revealed in the person of Jesus Christ, it is the person of the Spirit, the Spirit of God in Christ, who is the dynamic force that brings about the true communion of God and humanity.[133] This critical retrieval of the doctrine of *perichoresis* does have the potential to restore the balance between Christ and the Spirit in our ecclesial praxis as we hold together autonomy and heteronomy, and unity and diversity as one reality. It is the Spirit who is the source of individuation and community, of autonomy and relation. The Spirit gathers together in Christ those who would not otherwise gather. In John 17:20-26, Jesus prays for the believers that they may be one in the Father and the Son and express their unity in love. The Spirit makes possible the true *perichoretic* union, makes possible unity amid diversity, without abolishing otherness or individuality. The Holy Spirit incorporates humanity and all of creation into the mystery of the dynamism of the mutual indwelling of being.[134] Through the indwelling of God, all creatures are mutually related and exist in communion. The deeper our communion with God, self, and others, the more we move into the fullness of our humanity. This achievement of communion—what we often refer to as *koinonia*—is consistent with a view of communion through a lens of the new cosmology, in which we celebrate "Trinitarian interconnectedness" in all of creation.[135]

Within this view of reality, Johnson's use of the term *asymmetrical otherness* offers a way to maintain God's otherness and ultimacy, as well as the two main feminist agendas noted in Chapter 3. Johnson's concern for symmetrical and asymmetrical relations emerges out of a feminist consciousness that offers alternative concepts of justice and the socio-political framework. She shows how the classical theistic models of "mutual coinherence" maintain what feminists call "inauthentic praxis," in that they uphold patriarchal and exclusionary practices that do not promote the full personhood of women in either the Western or Eastern churches.[136] In her view, the theistic models favour the radical independence between the infinite God and the finite world, in which the merely transcendent God has no real relation to the created realm.

Johnson is also critical of pantheistic models of "mutual coinherence" in which the infinite God is embedded in the finite world, thus denying any independence and freedom in the created world. The pantheistic model of divine immanence results in a lack of differentiation between God and the world, making no true relation possible. Johnson offers an alternative model of mutual coinherence that is "panentheistic." In pantheism, God *is* all things, while according to panentheism God is *in* all things. Johnson's panentheistic model preserves the radical distinction between God and the world and promotes God's "asymmetrical otherness in relations of reciprocity and mutuality."[137] In a panentheistic doctrine of *perichoresis*, God is both immanent and transcendent. God is in the world and the world is in God, yet each remains radically distinct and free.[138] The asymmetrical otherness is lived as relations of mutuality in which difference remains and is respected.

Johnson's theological inquiry starts with the stories of women's experience of the Spirit to ensure that women's experience is heard, reflected upon, and integrated into our ways of knowing God.

> By focusing on the Spirit as the starting point for her Trinitarian theology, Johnson seeks to redress the neglect of pneumatology [the theology of the Holy Spirit] in Western theology while also honoring an insight from women's experience, which prefers to begin from the experiential rather than from the speculative.[139]

This starting point is also coherent with our Judeo-Christian tradition, in which doctrine is an expression of the human experience of salvation. In the Spirit we come to know God in Christ, "through whom we are joined with all humanity, all creation; and with the ultimate Source of our origin."[140]

Panentheism, together with the experience of the Spirit as the starting point for our theological discourse, opens the possibility for female metaphors for God, especially in the form of maternal and friendship imagery.[141] Panentheism provides a theoretical base for ecofeminist spirituality, in which God is "the creative force in the universe and a dynamic presence within every nook and cranny of creation."[142] The fundamental vision of mutual coinherence, in which divine relatedness to the world overcomes the isolation of a patriarchal God, is congruent with feminist values of mutuality and reciprocity.[143] This understanding of *perichoresis* deconstructs the dominant power relations of hierarchical patriarchy in our ecclesial and social praxis and contributes to a theological framework for moving toward a more inclusive church.

Koinonia

The Greek word *koinonia* has its roots in Greek philosophy, "especially in Plato, who understood it as a life-giving participation in the eternal realities."[144] Christians have traditionally translated *koinonia* as "community" or "communion." The ground of *koinonia* is located in the very being of God, which is first and foremost relational. As the doctrine of *perichoresis* has developed over the centuries, it has defined and given meaning to the lived experience of *koinonia* of the first Christians. For the early church, *koinonia* was lived as both a participation in divine nature (2 Peter 1:4) and a social responsibility "to 'share in the needs of the saints' (Rom. 12-13)."[145] The *perichoretic* life of our Christian God is a dynamic and energetic existence that invites us to live in *koinonia* with each other and with God. The energy of this communion is both the life *of* God and life *in* God. This is evidenced in the story of Pentecost, in which the community of disciples was confirmed with the striking symbols of wind and fire. From that experience, the disciples went forth to preach the gospel; as a result of their preaching, new communities emerged throughout the known world.[146]

The Second Vatican Council reclaimed this ancient concept of *koinonia* as a fundamental expression of church.[147] In faithfulness to the conciliar call to *ressourcement* and *aggionormento*, we continue to develop the concept of *koinonia* in keeping with the critical issues of our times. One of those current issues is the ecological crisis. Most people have some degree of concern for the preservation of our environment. In moving toward a more inclusive church, we seek to address that concern as a people of faith. As we look to the richness of our Christian tradition, we discover that an even deeper understanding of *koinonia* moves us to extend communion not only to all human beings but also to "other living creatures, ecosystems, and the whole natural world itself."[148]

As with *perichoresis*, recovering our understanding of community as *koinonia* rebalances the Christ-Spirit poles of Trinitarian theology and developing ecclesiologies. The Western tendency toward individualism in ontology, and its desire to treat Christology as an autonomous subject, has separated ministry and ordination, leading to the two-tiered structure of cleric-lay relations. A critical retrieval of *koinonia* as intrinsic to a Trinitarian theology of relationship opens the way to rediscover that ordination and the public mandating of pastoral leaders are acts that constitute community.[149] It is the work of the Spirit to achieve *koinonia* by creating and maintaining diversity-in-unity. This is the autopoietic energy that both differentiates and unites.

The Trinity's *koinonia* is the ground and goal of all relations of communion. In *koinonia*, power is shared as the partners partake in the life of community as subjects. In *koinonia*, difference does not lead to subordination, but rather expands and enriches inter-subjective relations of mutuality and reciprocity. The concept of *koinonia* is extended into the next chapter in my proposal for developing ecclesiologies.

Conclusion

Engaging in Trinitarian theology can be messy work. Some readers might wince at the monarchical and patriarchal language found in both the Western and Eastern Trinitarian doctrines. Others might cringe at some of the newer attempts to express an image of God that does not connect with their experience.[150] I consider it to be both a privilege and a responsibility to critically retrieve and discerningly work with emerging God-concepts that offer expanded and complex understandings of relationship with God, self, church, others, and world. Trinitarian doctrine stands as a profound critique of ecclesial praxis. Inauthentic ecclesial praxis reveals an abstract, patriarchal view of God that perpetuates isolationist practices, dualisms, and subject-object relations. In a dualistic view of reality, ontology is separated from and valued over function, essence over energies, cleric over lay, spirit over body, masculine over feminine, transcendent over immanent, and universal over particular.

A Trinitarian theology of relationship for authentic ecclesial praxis transcends dualisms and reveals our deep interconnectedness in God with all of creation. A doctrine marked by *perichoresis* and *koinonia* upholds an ecclesial praxis of mutuality, partnership, collegiality, co-responsibility, communion, and love, in which genuine difference among persons is a precondition to communion. As a people of faith, we know that true communion is never fully realized but rather is an eschatological hope. Christian hope is a hope concerning the world. "The praxis of the transforming mission calls for a certain worldview; one that carries a trust and hope concerning the world."[151] If we as disciples claim to be part of the transforming mission of Jesus Christ in the world, then we must be seekers of God *in* the world. Our ecclesial praxis must embody that hope.

5

Language and Vision of Church: Moving Toward a More Inclusive Church

Just as our social and historical context changes over time, so our ways of seeing and being church also evolve. During the first two centuries of Christianity, the early church structured its community life and ministries in an organic way. Until the Edict of Milan in 313 CE, Christians were a persecuted minority in the Roman Empire, where paganism was the mainstream religion. Christian identity and praxis were shaped by their location in the prevailing culture as well as by the needs of the context in which the particular churches developed. To this day, the conversion of the Roman Emperor Constantine in 311 CE is the most significant turning point in the historical development of Christianity.

Under Constantine's rule, the church experienced phenomenal growth. Christians became safe from persecution and their leaders gained favour with the emperor. However, many people were attracted to Christianity more because of wealth and favoured positions than the Christian mission. We can trace the cleric-lay divide back to the post-Constantinian church, in which baptism had "become a mere coincidence to citizenship."[152] Instead, ordination or religious vows became the ideal way to dedicate oneself to Christ's mission. As church and state became more and more integrated, the church's expansion prompted the building of specialized places of worship in which leaders were architecturally separated from the common attendees. These new structures stood in sharp contrast to the earlier house churches, which were local, small, and informal. These same new structures became symbolic of the beginning of the deep divide between the church's "official" leaders and the rest of the community. Here we see the growing separation being made between the baptized and the ordained as the church sought, often unsuccessfully, to maintain some kind of distinction between it and the economic-political sphere. Over time, the church continued to align its structures with the prevailing European autocratic regimes, in which there was a very clear distinction between the rulers and the followers.[153]

The time of Western autocracies is over. Even Western countries that maintain their monarchies have implemented some form of democratic structure in which all citizens have an equal voice somewhere in the decision-making process. With the rise of democracy, human rights and ecological concerns have received more attention in the mass media. The market-driven economy has come to have more influence on culture and social practices than our ecclesial or even political structures. In the 1960s, no longer able to ignore both the incremental and episodic changes taking place throughout the world, the church convened the Second Vatican Council, effectively opening the doors for imagining other ways of seeing and being church. A flurry of research and writing about change in ecclesiology has followed that event.

Developing visions of church

Ecclesiology is the study of the theological and practical questions that concern the organized Christian community. Those questions—which have been asked and are continuing throughout history—address the nature, purpose, patterns of authority and participation, boundaries, and central values of the Christian community.[154] As a branch of theology, ecclesiology is part of the living tradition of the church. The word *tradition* is often equated with stability and order; however, the adjective *living* helps us see that traditions, when vital, develop as they incorporate the changes brought about through ongoing difference and conflict. Therefore, tradition "is not a block of content to be carefully guarded by authorized hierarchies but a dynamic action of God's love which is to be passed on to others of all sexes and races."[155] As a bearer of tradition, the church's common life is constituted by the continuous disagreement on what it is and what it ought to be, between its practice and its vision. As both a divine and human institution, the church continues to write its not-yet-completed story, rooted in its past and attentive to the present.[156] As a member of this living tradition, I believe that the language we use to share and reflect on our personal and collective Christian stories has an important role to play in shaping our ways of seeing and being church based on a "still living and evolving past in order to shape a usable future."[157] It is in reflecting on our stories that we make claims and propose theories for the continuing life of our tradition.

Almost 50 years after Vatican II, we have not yet plumbed the depths of the richness of the conciliar documents, particularly as they affect our living tradition and ecclesial praxis. I bring your attention to two such documents: the Dogmatic Constitution of the Church, commonly known as *Lumen Gentium*, and the Pastoral Constitution on the Church in the Modern World (*Gaudium et Spes*). *Lumen Gentium*, which in English means "Light of all nations," deals specifically with the structure and nature of the church: in particular its internal dimension and relationships. *Gaudium et Spes* ("Joy and Hope") addresses the church's mission in the world, in particular the external or outer dimension and relationships. As the names of these documents suggest, each reflects a radical reorientation of the church's self-understanding and its relationship with the world.

In *Lumen Gentium*, the church shifts from identifying itself as a perfect society in which only those inside have access to God's reign, to becoming a sign, a sacrament of God's reign and presence to the world. In *Gaudium et Spes*, the church moves from an attitude of fear and mistrust of the world, to becoming a seeker of "authentic signs of God's presence and purpose" in the world.[158] Furthermore, *Gaudium et Spes* emphasizes that our seeking is to be done in a genuine spirit of hope, celebrating God's creativity and goodness, and lamenting the power of sin that oppresses and dehumanizes.[159] While all sixteen conciliar documents reflect on essential aspects of the church and its mission, *Lumen Gentium* and *Gaudium et Spes* are foundational for all ecclesiologies today.

We live in a time in which the clear demarcation between what we consider inner and outer is less and less obvious. Until the mid-twentieth century, women and children were traditionally considered part of the private domain of the household, while men were associated with the public domain of economic and political life. In the Western world, that is no longer the norm. Our inner life is intrinsically related to the way we act in the world at large Our family life—often considered a private domain—has immense implications on our public life as citizens, and vice versa. Feminism has enabled us to recognize the importance of public decision in matters that have been deemed part of the private world of women and family. For example, concern for adequate child care and for children's and women's rights has opened the way for public debate and policy-making. We have come to see that human beings develop in social webs that are deeply formative. As citizens, we all share responsibility for public behaviours and politics, since they have a significant influence on whether a person will develop to his or her fullest potential. Social policies flow from and into our private lives. As individuals and collectivities, our choices and actions are directly connected to our internal meaning-making and emotional systems.

In the previous chapter, I claimed that we cannot detach our being-for-one-another from our discourse of God's being and God's being-for-us. In a Trinitarian theology of relationship, God's intra-divine relations are distinct from God's presence and activity in the world, yet form one reality. If we limit our Trinitarian theology to God's inner life, we maintain God's absolute transcendence and keep God unrelated to history. As we shift toward an image of God characterized by *perichoresis* and *koinonia*, we come to see that God's radical transcendence is otherness, not remoteness, and God's radical immanence is God's nearness to us in history. We grasp God's very mystery as "transcendent because God's nearness to us in history does not exhaust the ineffable mystery of God."[160] This same God is calling us to rise above the conventional disconnect between church's inner life and its presence and activity in the world.

When we hold together God's immanence and radical otherness, the division we make between the church's spiritual community and its visible social structure becomes artificial. As *Lumen Gentium* claims, the church's divine and human elements "form one complex reality."[161] Just as our Trinitarian doctrine affirms Jesus Christ's nature as both human and divine, the Body of Christ is both human and divine. With eyes of faith, the human and divine are distinct yet together are one. The church's social structures serve the Spirit of Christ who in turn "promotes the body's growth in building itself up in love" (Ephesians 4:16).[162] In order to accomplish its mission, the church must grow. As a human structure, it is neither static nor fixed for eternity. It is, in its very nature, to continue to evolve in faithfulness to its mission in our changing environment. Ecclesiologist Avery Cardinal Dulles captures the urgency and imperative of our need to "read the signs of the times." In his seminal work *Models of the Church,* Dulles argues that if the church is to carry out its mission effectively, it must "enter into vigorous dialogue with the new world that is being born before our eyes."[163] Furthermore, he insists that if the church refuses to adapt as the times require, "it will become an ossified remnant of its former self."[164]

The evolutionary concepts of energy and system offer us a channel through which to receive Dulles's wisdom and see the church as a self-organizing system in which change is coherent with its ultimate calling or mission. In its bid for self-preservation, the church can choose eventual death as a closed system, or it can pay attention and creatively use the feedback it receives from its inner and outer environments. With eyes of faith looking through the lens of the new cosmology, we can see the Spirit of the Risen Christ in the autopoietic energy that calls and guides the church in the ways of truth from within, through the continual process of renewal and reconstruction. As change occurs and the church self-transcends in faithfulness to its calling, our movement toward greater inclusivity becomes more complex. As *Lumen Gentium* states, the Spirit dwells both in the church and in the hearts of the faithful, guiding the church in the way of all truth, bestowing upon it hierarchic and charismatic gifts, constantly rejuvenating and renewing it.[165] This same truth is articulated in another Vatican II document, the *Decree on Ecumenism,* in which the council says,

> Every renewal of the church essentially consists of an increase of fidelity to her own calling. Undoubtedly, this explains the dynamism of the movement toward unity. Christ summons the church, as she goes her pilgrim way, to that continual reformation of which she always had need, insofar as she is a human institution here on earth.[166]

In this change process, the church passes from its self-understanding as a static structure based on the certitude of possessing the truth to a communion in which "the unity of the church is always before us."[167] This call to unity is the source and goal of our mission. Unity, however, is not uniformity or sameness. The story of the Tower of Babel reveals this reality. When we impose our own unique brand of certitude on the world, we make it our god (Genesis 10 and 11).

Our ways of seeing and being church also cannot be reduced to a single concept. For many of us, this truth is evident in our experience of church. *Lumen Gentium* opens the way for a new vision of church that embraces both its unity and its diversity. With its focus on the mystery of the church and the people of God, *Lumen Gentium* acknowledges that the basic reality of the church is the mystery of God's presence within the entire community of the people of God. That same document addresses the church as hierarchy only in the third chapter, after it has covered the mystery of the church and the people of God. Here, the hierarchical structure is described as a "variety of offices which aim at the good of the whole body."[168] In this new vision, the key term is *collegiality,* as we move from placing heavy emphasis on the hierarchical and juridical aspects of the church to placing more importance on the church's vitality and dynamism as biblical and historical reality. Although the phrase *people of God* is not new to the Judeo-Christian tradition, its inclusion in *Lumen Gentium* opened the way for developing more inclusive ecclesiologies, all of which fit within the very broad framework of communion ecclesiology.

Vision of church as communion

Church as communion is a multidimensional ecclesial category that has in some ways become a catch-all for many expressions of Christian community today. Some of those visions either stress or hold in tension what continue to be the divisive poles of the institutional and charismatic, the christological and pneumatological, the mystical and socio-historical, as well as the human and divine aspects of the church.[169] In our history, we have tended to align the institutional with the christological, mystical, and divine elements of church, in contrast to the charismatic, pneumatological, socio-historical, and human elements. This bias exacerbates the separation we make between church and world, sacred and profane, body and spirit, and male and female. It also justifies benevolent paternalism and shields the church from charges of clericalism and clerical abuse.

The type of communion ecclesiology that I believe is best suited for living our mission today transcends those tensions by placing relationship at the centre of all things. As ecclesiologist Dennis Doyle states, "the Church is a web of interwoven relationships."[170] Cletus Wessels echoes that same claim when he refers to the church as a "Holy Web" of relationships. The relationships to which both Doyle and Wessels refer extend beyond the human and divine to include all of creation. The web consists of realities both visible and invisible, and both past and present, and on into the future. Just as in a Trinitarian theology of relationship, both autonomy and community—unity and diversity—co-exist as one reality in this view of church. It is the Spirit who makes true union possible, without abolishing otherness or individuality. The principles of *koinonia and perichoresis* lie at the heart of a communion ecclesiology that has its source and summit in the triune God.

The community of disciples is a variant of the communion model of church. Although the actual phrase *community of disciples* does not appear in the Vatican II documents, church members are referred to as disciples more than 20 times. Fewer than fifteen years after the close of the Second Vatican Council, Pope John Paul II used this same phrase in his encyclical *Redemptoris Hominis* to capture the complex reality of the personal and communal dimension of Christian calling. Relationship is at the heart of a community of disciples that self-consciously transcends the artificial distinction between its inner life as an assembled community and its mission in the world.[171]

In my experience, the creation of the Centre for Ministry Formation at Saint Paul University has opened the way for incarnating a community of disciples model of church. It has intentionally sought to put relationship at the heart of its efforts to move from an elitist view of ordained ministry to a view of ministry that has co-discipleship as its defining mark.[172] In its praxis, the Centre has attempted to move beyond the clerical elitism of "the Club"[173] mentality and offer formation that honours mutuality and solidarity in ministry. I use such terms as *efforts* and *attempts* because we often encounter paradox and contradictions in moving toward the unity and inclusivity to which the Spirit of Christ calls us. The language of "the Club" is powerful. Although I have heard this term used in reference to the church, I have actually borrowed it from an article by Michael Papesh, a Roman Catholic priest in the United States. In the article, he names the powerlessness of members of the clergy to free themselves from the clerical structure so that they may realize their commitment to move away from "the Club." He looks to lay people and the church at large to "ponder deeply our theology of ministry" and to radically critique elements of our ecclesial culture that render us ineffective today.[174]

There are times when we give lip service to the fact that "the Club" is no longer a model of church for today. Yet, there is much evidence that "the Club" continues to be well supported by an ingeniously designed anthropological, philosophical, theological, and ecclesiological system, which keeps us from moving toward a more inclusive church. Saying goodbye to "the Club" is complex and difficult work. It is not simply about improving ecclesial relations by goodwill or by legislating change among its members. It is also not simply about proposing a new paradigm of church in which those relations are modified. Instead, we must intentionally move toward a more inclusive church in a way that transforms relations and structures grounded in the critical correlation between our experience and developing theories of God, church, humankind, and the universe. This is transformative work. This kind of change cannot take place without surfacing and critiquing the assumptions that make up our systems of meaning that consciously or unconsciously narrow our choices and behaviours. As I have claimed throughout this book and demonstrate in Chapter 6, the intentional use of language can be a powerful force for the ongoing development of consciousness and deep structural change.

Models of church

Each model of church is an ordered system composed of a coherent body of social attitudes and teachings about the organization of authority in the community of faith, and about its mission. Authoritative tradition and power relations are significant theological issues that must be addressed in all models of church. I address these issues separately as well as in my exploration later in this chapter of two discipleship models of church that give us elements to consider in moving toward a more inclusive church: discipleship of equals, and holarchical church. These proposals—the first by Elizabeth Schüssler Fiorenza and the second by Cletus Wessels—share a deep conviction that the church is unfolding and emerging out of the presence of God within it. As I do, Fiorenza and Wessels build on the insights and visions of other theologians who call into question contemporary "well-orchestrated attempts to restore the church to the cultural ghetto opposition-to-the-world mentality of the pre-Council times."[175] There is no golden or ideal past to which to escape the immanent attraction to the future. With eyes of faith, we are called to freely trust the church's inherent capacity to self-organize according to its own calling and mission to participate in the vision of God's ultimate reign of love, peace, and justice in this world. Although the church may emerge in unanticipated ways, its fundamental vision is manifested in its authoritative tradition, which serves as a reference in guiding the church in its continuous renewal.

Authoritative tradition

Apostolicity is the most-cited authoritative tradition by which theologians authenticate Christian praxis. As with parts of the previous chapter on Trinitarian doctrine, readers may find this section on apostolicity rather technical. For that reason, I debated whether to include it. I came to the conclusion that if I left it out, readers might be left wondering where authoritative tradition fits in my vision of a changing church. For this reason, I invite readers to bear with me as I try to make the overall principle of apostolicity a little more user-friendly.

Dating back to the earliest of Christian communities, apostolicity has been considered a "distinguishing mark of the community as being discipleship of Jesus in teaching and lifestyle."[176] Unfortunately, the term *apostolicity* is often reduced to referring only to the apostolic succession of leadership in the church. While the succession of leaders is an aspect of apostolicity, it is but one part of the deeper vision of the "Christ event"[177] that directs and shapes the church's identity and praxis. As part of the living tradition of the church, apostolicity as the Christ-event is expressed and systematized in history, yet is not limited to a particular space and time. Edward Schillebeeckx offers a multidimensional model of apostolicity rooted in the life and mission of the Christian communities as they developed in their socio-historical contexts.

The first and most essential dimension of apostolicity is that the church is founded and built up on the story of the experience of apostles and prophets. For the earliest Christian communities, apostolicity was first and foremost the Gospel of Jesus Christ as it was told and reflected upon by the apostles and prophets.[178] Moving beyond first-generation Christianity, the post-apostolic leaders were concerned with preserving apostolic heritage. The ministry of these pastoral leaders was a "special ministerial charisma in the service of the community."[179]

The second aspect of apostolicity is the apostolic content of tradition that deals with the early church's concern for an "unbroken succession in teaching."[180] Here, the Gospels and the New Testament writings serve as permanent foundational documents. The central concern of the pastoral epistles (such as Paul's letters to the Corinthians, as well as the letters written by Peter, Timothy, James, etc.) is safeguarding the apostolic tradition, not the forms of ministry. According to Schillebeeckx, there must always be ministry in the church for the sake of the continuity of the apostolic teaching, particularly the New Testament mandate to "Do this in memory of me." It is the continuity of the apostolic teaching, not the maintenance of particular structures or forms of ministry, that ensures the community's apostolic identity.[181]

The third element is the apostolicity of the Christian communities of believers, in which the division between the community's inner relations and mission is transcended. These communities have been called to life by the apostles and prophets, based on the apostolic content of faith. Their main concern is the praxis of God's reign,[182] which consists of following Jesus in his message, in his teaching, and in his actions. Here, ministry is organic, diverse, and "clearly incorporated into the totality of all kinds of services which are necessary for the community itself."[183]

The fourth and final dimension of apostolicity is apostolic succession. If we use the pastoral epistles as our reference for this dimension, we will find no standards for how ministry must be structured and differentiated. The only norm is that ministry is necessary for any faith community, yet it is only one of many factors at the service of the apostolicity of the community.[184] In the earliest Christian communities, the laying on of hands was not a sign of the transference of ministerial authority. Rather, it was a ritual gesture of bestowing the charisma of the Holy Spirit in order "to help the minister to hand down and preserve in a living way the pledge entrusted to him and to make him able to proclaim the apostolic tradition intact."[185] Ministry was and continues to be connected with a special concern for the preservation of Christian identity of the community in constantly changing circumstances. Because the community itself is apostolic, the community has the responsibility to examine the apostolic foundation of its pastoral leaders.[186]

When we take a close look at the Roman Catholic Rite of Ordination, which was revised after the Second Vatican Council, we notice that when the candidate is presented, the bishop asks, "Do you judge him to be worthy?" The presenter responds, "After inquiry among the people of Christ and upon recommendation of those concerned with his training, I testify that he has been found worthy."[187] Although the rite does not define all that is meant by the term *worthy*, the apostolic faith of the candidate is an integral aspect of his worthiness. In this part of the rite, the presenter is seen to affirm the apostolic faith of the candidate for ordination. However, because the rite explicitly calls for the presenter to be a priest who is designated by the bishop, one could be forgiven for interpreting this part of the rite as an affirmation of being worthy for belonging to "the Club."[188] A more generous and intentional reading of the rite could see the presenter as testifying on behalf of the whole community. In the Byzantine Catholic Rite, the community's role in affirming the candidate's apostolic faith is evident in the singing of "*Aksios!*" (Greek for "He is worthy").

As these rites reveal, the very foundation for apostolic succession is the community of faith, whose role it is to determine the apostolic faith of its leaders and ministers. However, this reality is less evident in our actual praxis, which tends to disconnect ordained ministry from the very community that engenders its ministries. Ministry is just as important and necessary today as it ever was to preserve and keep alive the Gospel of Jesus Christ.[189] However, just as we tend to reduce apostolicity to "apostolic succession" so, too, we limit ministry to the structure of the ordained ministry of bishop, priest, and deacon. As our developing story shows, changes in the forms of ministry "appear as a consequence of social changes in the church and the world: the rise of a new spirituality, different views of church, society and the world."[190] While various forms of lay ministry are gaining more recognition today, they continue to be defined in terms of what they are not: ordained ministry.[191] Depending on how we read the "signs of the times," we can see change occurring in response to the stirrings of the Spirit, which is beckoning us to recognize new possibilities in moving toward a more inclusive church.

Structures of power relations

In our Christian vision of reality, God, world, and church are inextricably interconnected. Throughout Christian history, the prevailing models of church have been deeply rooted and shaped by their socio-historical contexts. Each of those contexts embodies a particular image of God, which is integrally related to the predominant world view of the time. Change in our ways of seeing and being church calls for attending to and critiquing our images of God that shape our religious consciousness and our structures of power relations. An image of God as an autonomous, transcendent, interventionist sovereign, relating from above and outside of creation, shapes a model of church as an ecclesial autocracy. Ecclesial autocracy is clericalism. Clericalism is the "management of ecclesiastical relationships in which everything goes from top to bottom."[192]

Clericalism is justified by subject-object relationships in which one group has the power and authority, and the other is led by the first. Here, God's power and authority are passed from the active subject, God the Father, to Jesus Christ, to the Holy Spirit, who in turn passes it on to the clergy (bishop, priest, deacon), who in turn pass it on to the laity, who in turn passes it on to the world. Within this network of relations, each person is a passive object in relation to what is above or before it, and each person is an active subject to what is below or after it. In this paradigm, lay people are passive objects until the clergy empowers them to be active in the world, and the world is a passive object waiting to be sanctified by the evangelizing presence of the church.[193] Because lay people are relegated to the field of the world, the cleric-lay divide informs relations both within the church as well as with the world.

Clericalism operates out of a mechanical view of energy in which work and control are the dominant themes. Here, potential energy is produced and distributed as a scarce resource. Clerics have control of the process of production in the church. God, sacraments, tradition, and moral teaching are the stored or potential energy ready to be changed into kinetic energy when the cleric works. Like the elite oil-producing consortium that controls the energy supply to most of the world, clerics structurally control the flow of *divine* energy into the world. The language we use to describe ordained ministry shows that our contemporary theology and praxis is very much informed by the cause-and-effect scheme of reality. Clerics are perceived as having the power to *bring* God to lay people; they *give* and *transmit* truth and God's compassion to the laity; they *administer* the sacraments. The laity simply receives what the cleric has the power to give. Clerics have control over the finished product. They have the power to verify whether a particular "practice, attitude or behaviour is truly 'of the church.'"[194] In clericalism, even though the language of "legitimate diversity"[195] is often used in place of *conformity*, the power to determine what falls outside the limit of legitimate diversity remains within the clerical structure.

The pattern of the cleric-lay relationship mirrors the structure that organizes our religious mentality, in which there is a deep divide between God/church and the world. That divide has serious consequences for our ability to choose and act as responsible Christians in the world today. Lay people are accustomed to receiving the truth of the world from the clergy. They are also accustomed to their mission being controlled by the clerics. They have learned to read the world in terms of what they have received from the top down. If we act as if God is a scarce resource or absent from the world until the church makes God present, then any attempts to live out our vocation as disciples will simply perpetuate inauthentic praxis. When we tamper with the internal logic that keeps that pattern in place, we risk destabilizing the very meaning structures through which we live out our historical relationships with God/church and world. However, when we intentionally reflect upon our faith experience and begin to critique our habitual frames of reference, we open ourselves to trying on other perspectives and other ways of expressing those perspectives.[196]

Evolutionary and feminist thought offer an alternative vision that transcends the cleric-lay divide, affirms the abundance of God's creativity and reveals the radical inclusivity of God's salvific presence. With new eyes of faith, we see God as both immanent and intentional, active in the limits and sinfulness of the world today. We hear God call all of creation into the co-creative act in a spirit of dynamism, collaboration, and interdependence.[197] Both Fiorenza and Wessels propose new ecclesial paradigms in which we move from God being mediated in a top-down fashion to God being at the "center of a web of relationships with the power and presence of God expanding in all directions from within."[198] In this image of God, the church moves from being "a clerico-pyramidal church to a church of communion."[199] Conformity and uniformity give way to originality, diversity, and unity. Earlier in this chapter, I referred to the story of the Tower of Babel as a way of interpreting the movement from uniformity to unity. This same biblical story also reveals our human tendency to build structures that lift us out of the ordinary realm of creaturely existence. As a brief commentary on that passage states, for the nomadic people, "the Mesopotamian city culture was characterized by the ziggurat, a pyramidal temple tower whose summit was believed to be the gateway to heaven, the realm of the gods."[200] This passage sheds light on our ecclesial praxis. We can compare the Mesopotamian city culture with the cleric-lay church that is epitomized by its own ziggurat, a uniform, pyramidal temple tower. When we read the "signs of the times," we might discover that this same church is being called to deconstruct its own pyramid and move toward greater diversity, unity, and inclusivity in its relations and in how it lives out its mission. This is the kind of change called for in moving toward a more inclusive church.

Like Schillebeeckx, both Fiorenza and Wessels agree that the church will always need ministry and leadership, even though the current structures in which ministry is exercised are no longer adequate. Both authors offer us a new language and new concepts to consider for transforming power relations and structures in moving toward a more inclusive church. Like Schillebeeckx, they are concerned with maintaining apostolicity in the broader sense than just apostolic succession. Although Fiorenza and Wessels use different foundations to support their arguments, they are equally intent on declericalizing the power structures. Their main objective is to transcend the dualisms between clergy and laity, as well as between the inner-directed ministries, which have been traditionally the domain of the clergy, and outer-directed ministries, which have traditionally been the reserve of the laity. I now draw upon some of those insights and offer them as possibilities for imagining new ways of seeing and being faithful to our mission in moving toward a more inclusive church.

Discipleship of equals

Fiorenza uses the phrase *discipleship of equals* to express her vision of a community of disciples in which all ministries are the right, responsibility, and vocation of all the baptized.[201] She proposes a psychological, theological and structural transformation of the Constantinian church, so that men and women have space to "attain full spiritual autonomy, power, self-determination and liberation."[202] The *discipleship of equals* stands as a corrective to the subject-object power relations in which clerics hold supra-historical decision-making authority.[203] Fiorenza's main goal is to declericalize the church, not to clericalize women or the laity.[204] Declericalization maintains the church's need for leadership and seeks renewed structures of ecclesial relations that are defined by mutuality, diversity, and inter-subjectivity. Fiorenza calls for the democratization of ministry, a call that is consistent with the experience of Pentecost. That founding event offers us a privileged view of God's salvific power and presence in the Upper Room, freely bestowing gifts and charisms on all who are gathered, for the good of God's holy people.

In her critical retrieval of the experience of the early church, Fiorenza offers us two terms that define the church's mission as well as its structure; *basileia* and *ekklesia*. *Basileia* is the "vision of God's alternative world, a vision of justice, human dignity, equality and salvation for all."[205] The *basileia* vision of the Gospels is at the heart of our apostolic heritage, since it constitutes the church's existence and mission. The disciples of the *basileia* share in the mission of the Risen Christ to proclaim and make present the reign of God, the good news of God's alternative world of justice and love. The early Christian term *ekklesia* expresses what Fiorenza means by a participatory-inclusive model of church[206] *Ekklesia* is the full decision-making, democratic assembly of free citizens in the early Christian movement. Within the *ekklesia*, "ministry is a function of the whole people of God vis-à-vis the whole world."[207]

In this discipleship of equals model of church, *basileia* and *ekklesia* incorporate the Galatians 3:28 vision of church in which "there is no longer Jew or Greek, there is no longer slave or free, there is no longer male and female; for all of you are one in Christ Jesus." As with all scripture passages, Galatians 3:28 has been interpreted in a number of ways. The church has tended to see it as being purely charismatic, calling our faith communities to live as one loving family. While this approach is important, it is not enough. Fiorenza argues that this same passage must be seen as applying to the structure and organization of the Christian community.[208] Her use of the term *ekklesia* gives a structure to the Pauline understanding of community as *koinonia*, which provides a sacramental foundation for collegiality, co-responsibility, consensual as well as ecumenical partnership, and mission to the world.[209] The *koinonia* partnership is lived out in unity and diversity. My experience of ministry in the Centre for Ministry Formation at Saint Paul University has given me a taste for living this kind of partnership. I have come to see that this vision is possible when the partners are in unity—not uniformity—with respect to their vision, purpose, and commitment, upon which the partnership was initially founded.

Holarchical church

Like Fiorenza, Wessels offers new language to express a new ecclesial paradigm for seeing and being church today. However, unlike Fiorenza, who finds her language in the richness of the tradition, Wessels seeks signs of God's presence in a more contemporary view of reality. Through the lens of the new cosmology, in which the theory of holons "describes the web of relationships in the universe,"[210] Wessels sees a call to become a "holarchical" church.[211] As we saw in Chapter 3, holarchy is a series of holons that are whole/parts. In this theory, reality is neither a whole nor a part, but simultaneously both. As whole/parts, holons have the capacity to develop horizontal relationships through self-preservation and self-adaptation. In holons, individuality and communion co-exist as one reality. As a whole, holons can preserve their own particular wholeness or autonomy. As a part, holons must adapt or accommodate themselves to other holons. Holons exemplify mutuality in that "the parts exercise a control over the larger whole, but the whole also exercises control over the constituent parts."[212] Holons also have the capacity for self-transcendence and for self-dissolution. Self-transcendence increases the holon's vertical or hierarchical ordering through transformation to a higher order of complexity. Self-transcendence is the "capacity to reach beyond the given and introduce some measure of novelty."[213] Holons can also break down. When they dissolve, they tend to do so along the same vertical sequence in which they were built.

Holarchy has a "wide range of application, from organisms to language to social systems."[214] Some theologians claim that the principle of holarchy is so pervasive in all of reality that it seems to be a "universal structure of created being."[215] When we use eyes of faith, holarchy can offer us a lens for changing our ways of seeing and being church. Through this lens, the church shows that it has the same four capacities as whole/parts described above. Throughout its history, the church has made changes to preserve itself, as well as to adapt to the evolving culture. The Constantinian church exemplifies this capacity. The church also shows itself to be capable of self-transcendence, most recently in the Second Vatican Council. It is also capable of dissolution. Although it may never completely dissolve, it has already dissipated for some communities and for individuals who have found the church to be more destructive than life-giving. My grandfather and his family lived an acute experience of dissolution, as did the Roman Catholic Church in Quebec, when the close alignment of the socio-political with the religious structures began to unravel in the 1960s.

Although holons are intrinsically hierarchical as well as horizontal, the language of hierarchy is too often equated with command and autocracy in both society and religion. For this reason, Wessels suggests we change our conventional language of hierarchy to holarchy to express the church's capacity to grow and change in its height as well as its depth and span.[216] In a holarchical church, there is no one master controller who passes down authority to the one below him. It is a community of disciples, a "holy web" of relationships in which all members are subjects and all are disciples, all are hearers, all are listeners, all are learners. The holarchical church "is a self-organizing system [that] unfolds and emerges out of the presence of God within it."[217] It embodies the *koinonian* vision of ecclesial relations marked by *perichoretic* relations of diversity, mutuality, subjectivity, interdependence, and communion.

If we see the church as a self-organizing system, then we see pastoral leadership as called to create an environment for collective leadership in which all learn to become more and more capable of participating in the unfolding of the church. Pastoral leadership essentially frees the community to "discover the internal movement and guidance of the Creator Spirit."[218] This calls for listening to what wants to emerge in the life of God's people "and then having the courage to do what is required."[219] In a holarchical church, there is a deep connection between the community and its leaders. It needs pastoral leaders who are called, competent, and affirmed by the community. That affirmation would be a form of pastoral institutionalization as a means of ensuring its apostolicity. Like Fiorenza, Wessels suggests ways to declericalize the church. In his view, declericalization aims to remedy the "fallacious and perverse power that gives clerics a tranquil prepossession of the truth."[220] It does not mean that we do not need pastoral leaders, since without them, the community risks losing its apostolicity. However, perhaps it is time to look at other configurations and structures for mandating, commissioning, or ordaining pastoral leaders. The current form of ordained ministry—bishop, priest, and deacon—was developed in response to concerns in other times and places.[221] That structure is not fixed for eternity. This could be the time to imagine other possibilities, to open ourselves to embracing the diversity of ministries emerging in the life of the church. If we are truly committed to moving toward a more inclusive church, we must become more intentional in changing language that perpetuates clerical elitism in favour of a language of charism and gift, revealing ecclesial relations that are "egalitarian, yet differentiated, mutual and reciprocal."[222]

In Papesh's plea for transforming "the Club," he sees clerics as powerless captives to a system that has lost its capacity to live out its mission in a life-giving and authentic manner.[223] Wessels sees reality a little differently. In his view, both laity and clergy can be either oppressed or free. However, oppression can be transformed through freedom and choice. People can choose not to be in top-down, subject-object relationships. In a holarchical church, the only true freedom is the freedom "that comes from within, when the oppressed choose to be free."[224] In Wessels's view, wherever there is oppression in the church, freedom will come when laity choose to cease being laity and clergy choose to cease being clergy. While I agree with Wessels that "to live out such a new paradigm will require a deep and strong faith in the presence and power of God,"[225] it would be naive to think that we can achieve this kind of freedom without concerted, intentional effort. Unless we intentionally surface and critique our assumptions that keep us from making the change to which we are truly committed, it will be nearly impossible to live out this new paradigm.

Conclusion

While some may find Fiorenza's and Wessels's models of church a rather large stretch of the imagination, they offer us some important elements to consider in moving toward a more inclusive church. Both these community of disciples models call Christians to a level of maturity in which co-reponsibility and co-discipleship are the defining marks of Christian life and ecclesial relations. Wessels's prescription for change is radical and alluring. His proposal that clerics cease to be clerics and lay people cease to be lay people cannot happen without transformational change. Not only do we have a long history of cleric-lay relations, and deeply ingrained cleric and lay identities, we have an ingeniously designed theological system and ecclesial practice in which stability and order continue to be of primary concern. Neither coercion nor censure of exclusive behaviour serves long-term transformation, attitudes, and ministerial identity. New ecclesial relations call for deep structural change. Without this kind of change, neither laity nor clerics are free to choose to change their behaviours or attitudes. Any possibility of deep structural change calls for opportunities for self-awareness and critiquing our meaning-making structures. In the following chapter, I show how the "immunity-to-change language technology" can be a mechanism for enabling that depth of change.

6

Language and Change: Working with "Immunity-to-change"[226]

> "If we want deeper understanding of the prospect of change, we must pay closer attention to our own powerful inclinations not to change."[227]

The language we use can be a vital means for change in our faith communities. When we identify our faith communities—parishes, congregations, classrooms, even families—as language communities, we can intentionally shape the language in that environment. What we speak expresses our fundamental values and ideals, some of which can only come into existence through the language we choose to express them. This conviction has formed my own life and ministry. In my family, we encouraged or discouraged certain kinds of language. For example, my husband and I discouraged our children from using language that was disrespectful or demeaning; we encouraged them to speak their truth in a way that affirmed and built up the other. I carried this same sensibility into my ministry in the Centre for Ministry Formation. There, we encouraged people to use language that expresses a dynamic and inclusive view of church and world in which we claimed our identities as co-disciples. We discouraged language that upholds the subject-object polarity.

For example, rather than calling the candidates for ordained ministry "seminarians" and all the others "candidates for lay ministry," all the Centre members were considered candidates for ministry: some for lay ministry and some for ordained ministry. This language expresses the equal dignity and multiplicity of ministries, and yet does not lose sight of difference. We intentionally identified and shaped the Centre as a community of adult learners using a language of invitation and partnership rather than one of obligation and submission to a particular set of predetermined regulations. This new language invited us into a new way of becoming church in which all persons are subjects—hearers, listeners, and co-disciples in Christ's mission. Yet *what* we speak is not enough. While the language we use to express our concerns and values can construct what is real and true for us,[228] transformational change can take place only when we change the form of our knowing.

Mental Structures

As we saw in Chapter 1, our forms of knowing are the mental structures that shape the meaning we give to reality. Our values and sense of self are anchored in our forms of knowing. They provide us with a sense of stability, coherence, community, and identity. Who we are and what we value are deeply interconnected. That is why we might react to questions about our values as personal attacks. That is also why we might dismiss alternative viewpoints that call our ways of knowing into question as "distorting, deceptive, ill-intentioned or even crazy."[229]

During much of our lives, we make meaning by integrating new experiences into what we already know. This often works well for us, especially when we engage in routine tasks. However, when significant questions arise out of our lived experience, our frames of reference might no longer fit. Our habitual patterns for determining what is real and true can be challenged, even threatened. In order to avoid the chaos of the unknown, we either try to fit these new experiences into what we already know, or we dismiss, or, worse yet, deny their truth.

As I reflect on my experience as a pastoral associate in a local parish, I can see how I at times denied the truth of my experience. Although I was an integral part of the pastoral leadership of the community in which I served, I was at times virtually invisible. At one Easter Vigil, I found myself weeping at the back of the church, feeling very much alone and excluded from the community in which I had partnered to prepare for this important celebration. Although my feelings were giving me important signs about the pain of separation I was living as a lay pastoral associate, I unconsciously chose to fit that experience into my habitual meaning structures, in which the lay–cleric divide justified why I was hidden at the back of the church. This viewpoint is well anchored in our current reality, in which the church simultaneously seeks more lay participation and upholds the power structure of a two-caste system.[230]

After that celebration, I resumed my normal way of acting as a lay pastoral associate, giving little thought to what I had lived at that time. It took me a couple of years to share that experience with someone. By listening and asking me questions, she helped me become aware of my way of making meaning, which I had taken as true. Her carefully formulated questions opened the way for me to critique my own assumptions and imagine other possibilities. This was a major learning for me! Until that time, I myself did not realize that when we are unaware of our own meaning-making structures, we are unconscious of how they constrict the choices we make in our ways of judging and acting.

I have since grown to appreciate how careful questioning can jar us out of our unconscious habits and unleash energy that begins to move us away from the meaning structures that hold us captive to repetitive behaviours undermining even our most sincere commitments to change. This energy differentiates us from our habitual patterns of defining reality so that we may look *at* rather than *through* our forms of knowing. My own personal learning is deeply connected with my ministry in the Centre for Ministry Formation. There I discovered that if we are intentional about *how* we speak, we can open up possibilities for examining and even changing the form of our knowing so that what we speak fits with our vision. For example, the language of invitation and partnership does not fit into a mental structure that maintains the subject-object polarity of church and world, nor does it fit into an image of God that is exclusively patriarchal, hierarchical, and transcendent.

With eyes of faith, we can see how our forms of knowing are intrinsically related to realizing our mission in Christ. In becoming conscious of our forms of knowing—our mental structures through which we make meaning—we can become freer to engage in God's call to the fullness of life. In their call to all of God's people to be a holy people, the Levitical priests knew this to be true. They write:

> I will walk among you and be your God and you shall be my people. I am the Lord your God who brought you out of the land of Egypt, to be their slaves no more. I have broken the bars of your yoke and made you walk erect. (Leviticus 26:12-13)

This timeless text addresses Christians today: We are God's people. God calls; we respond. God invites us into the co-creative act, of partnering *with* God to free ourselves from the structures of oppression that keep us from fulfilling our vocation as people and communities of faith. My own story testifies to this truth. It also gives evidence to the fact that we cannot free ourselves alone. We need people and resources to help us to examine and transform our forms of knowing as we respond to God's invitation to freely embrace the dynamism of life.

Adult Development Theory

The "immunity-to-change language technology" is based on Robert Kegan's constructive-developmental approach to adult development and object relations theory.[231] Constructive-development theory builds on Piaget's constructivist theory of child and adolescent development. In this theory, human development is marked by a continuous movement between autonomy and inclusion into increasingly more complex and inclusive orders of consciousness. Orders of consciousness are the mental structures that organize and regulate our thinking, feeling, and ways of relating. In object-relations theory, the subject-object relationship is the "deep structure" of our mental organization.[232] While the language of "subject-object" may appear to contradict the call for overcoming the cleric–lay, church–world relations in moving toward a more inclusive church, it is a key concept in a constructivist approach to human development. Object refers to the elements of our knowing that we can reflect on and for which we can be responsible. An element of knowing is object to us when it is distinct enough from us that we can do something with it. Conversely, subject refers to the elements with which we are identified or in which we are embedded. We cannot reflect upon those elements to which we are subject. Because they are hidden from our awareness, they unconsciously regulate our thinking, feeling, and ways of relating. Subject is absolute; object is relative.

Until I was invited to reflect upon my Easter Vigil experience, I remained subject to my own form of knowing. The conventional cleric–lay relations absolutely defined what was real and true for me. It was only in being asked some very specific questions that I was able to look *at* that frame of reference and start asking my own questions. These questions opened the way for dis-embedding myself from my familiar way of meaning-making. Rather than looking *through* the cleric-lay structure, I began to see it as object to my knowing. I could then examine it and begin to question whether there was another way of seeing and being church today. Gradually, I discovered that I was co-responsible, that through my own choices and behaviours, I had some responsibility for perpetuating the structures that kept me invisible in the back of the church.

Deep Structural Change

Deep structural change is transformational change. It is change in the subject-object relationship of our mental structures. When we make our mental structures the object of our knowing, we increase our capacity to act and be responsible as free subjects. The "immunity-to-change language technology" is designed to disturb the inner logic that regulates our meaning-making structures. That inner logic is the hidden immune system that keeps us from making the change to which we are truly committed.

All humans have built-in "immune systems." In this context, we are referring not to our human biology but the internal forces that maintain equilibrium and make persons and organizations change-resistant. This simultaneous commitment to change and non-change is not a character flaw. It is a natural phenomenon. People's most sincere commitment to change is unconsciously undermined by our competing commitments, which maintain equilibrium. Individuals and organizations are instinctually pulled in multiple directions by competing commitments in order to preserve themselves from the threat of bringing into question their very systems of meaning. Even the best-intentioned people keep themselves from doing what it is they are genuinely committed to doing.[233]

Deep structural change is very different from a quick-fix solution. Many of us have had some experience with quick-fix programs in our lives, such as fad diets or exercise programs that quickly fizzle out. Once we stop the diet or exercise program, we often revert to our unhealthy behaviour. Why? Because we fail to go beyond surface change to discover what is really keeping us from making the change we desire. (Some people describe this behaviour as "rearranging the deckchairs on the Titanic"—it is pointless and, in some cases, potentially dangerous.) Communities also engage in quick-fix solutions that do not address deep structural change. Many of us have participated in parish renewal programs or synodal processes that have initially generated much energy for change, but have ended up going nowhere, as normal life resumes.

Deep structural change is change in our ways of knowing. It transforms our relation to the structures through which we make meaning. The first step toward deep structural change is to acknowledge that we all have a hidden immune system that maintains our simultaneous commitment to change and non-change. The next step is to seek out or create opportunities to disturb the inner logic of mental structures that keep our immune system intact. It is only in making our reality object that we can reflect on it, question it, and even test it so it no longer has an unconscious hold on us. While no change process carries any guarantee for success, these initial steps can prevent us from making easily reversible changes that bring us back to the status quo.

In Chapter 2, I cited Johnson's claim that "Linguistic change and structural change go hand in hand."[234] This is also true for change is our mental structures—deep structural change in our ways of knowing. However, the linguistic change that is required is not only the spoken word, but also our internal language. In other words, in our attempts to overcome our resistance to change, we must pay attention to "how we speak to *ourselves.*"[235] What we say to ourselves can be just as formative as what we say out loud. If the little voice inside my head keeps saying that I must be perfect in order to be acceptable, or that I must keep quiet in order to fit into the current cleric–lay relations, then I will continue to act out of that internal language. The same is true for our communities. What we say to ourselves within our communities is also deeply formative. For example, if candidates for ordained ministry speak an inclusive language when they are in community with all candidates for ministry, and an exclusive language when they are with only other candidates for ordained ministry or other ordained ministers, their language will reinforce the mentality of "the Club" as they act out of a narrower view of church and world.

Not only must we pay attention to what we say but we must also be attentive to the form of what we say. All language forms are powerful. They can either constrain or expand how we see the world and act in it.[236] They can either maintain or disturb the inner logic of our mental structures that regulate how we think, feel, and make meaning of our experiences. Some language forms can dissipate energy in a way that constricts our choices; others can concentrate more individual and social energy. The greater the concentration of energy, the greater the possibility of our ongoing development. For example, as you will see below, the language of complaint dissipates energy and can eventually lead to paralysis or breakdown. However, if we pay attention to those complaints, we can transform them into another language form, a language of commitment that is energizing and that opens up possibilities for creativity and renewal.

The diagnostic phase of the "immunity-to-change language technology" introduces us to novel language forms. In this phase, the four-column exercise (see appendices 1 to 4) offers us language forms as tools for transforming our habitual ways of making meaning. This language is aimed at unearthing competing commitments, which are the psychological dynamics of self-protection that make us immune to change.[237] Learning to use these language forms can be a process for people to develop greater consciousness of their competing commitments and to identify their big assumptions, which give rise to those same competing commitments and anchor the whole immunity-to-change system.[238] The big assumptions are systems of meaning that consciously or unconsciously affect our choices and behaviours. As the term suggests, the follow-up phase follows the diagnostic phase of the "immunity-to-change language technology." This second phase is designed as a time for people to engage in the messy work of disembedding themselves from their own systems of meaning, to objectify that which they hold as ultimate or absolute, in order that they may reflect on it and begin to question its validity.

My experience and research convince me that even our most sincere commitment to moving toward a more inclusive church will be undermined by our immunity to change. Unless we surface the personal and collective assumptions that keep us from moving from what Rémi Parent calls "the uniformity of a clerico-pyramidal church to a church of communion,"[239] the current cleric–lay separation will remain intact. The "immunity-to-change language technology" can be a way for us to respond to the gospel call to examine our own certitude and ways of making meaning of reality. In the Gospel of Matthew, Jesus tells us,

> The eye is the lamp of the body. So, if your eye is healthy, your whole body will be full of light, but if your eye is unhealthy, your whole body will be full of darkness. If then the light in you is darkness, how great is the darkness! (Matthew 6:22-24)

In this passage, the eye is the metaphor for our way of knowing, seeing, and being in the world. The way we see affects what is right and true for us. Throughout the Gospels, Jesus equates health with wholeness, light, and right relationship. An unhealthy eye has limited vision, which in turn limits our capacity to fully live out of our call to wholeness and right relationship. On the other hand, if our eyes are healthy, then our vision is clear and undistorted. When we see through healthy eyes, light can illuminate every corner of our hearts and minds. Nothing is left in darkness. Yet, darkness and light go hand in hand. Without the light, we cannot know darkness, and vice versa. The "immunity-to-change language technology" works with the learnings we have found in both the light and darkness. It helps us to take a deep look at our praxis—at the strengths and limits of what we do and don't do, as well as why. As you will see below, when we respond to the specific questions in each of the four columns with the utmost candour and truthfulness, we can begin to see why we make choices and act in ways that work against our true commitments. Unless we intentionally attend to and reflect on what we do, we risk simply repeating the same behaviours. When we allow ourselves to face and stay with the darkness of our competing commitments and big assumptions, we can mine and bring to light unspoken truths that keep us from making the change to which we are truly committed. We cannot do this work alone. This is the work of co-discipleship. It is in solidarity with our partners in Christ that we muster the courage and commitment to do this work so that we may freely live in God's gracious and generous abundance.

Diagnostic phase: Using different language forms

Enough talk about how language can facilitate change. Now it is time to practise it. I will now lead you through a four-column exercise that consists of four novel language forms: language of commitment, language of personal responsibility, language of competing commitment, and language of the big assumption we hold. In this exercise, we will use two examples of individual work (Dorothy and Michael) and one of collective work (St. Cloud Pastoral Leadership Team). Using the same examples, I will also show how intentionally structured follow-up work can be a time for reflecting on and changing the inner logic that anchors our immunity to change. At the end of the book, I have included four appendices with some practical guidelines and a step-by-step process for facilitating the four-column exercise and follow-up work for both individuals and groups. I suggest that you review those appendices closely before actually using the four-column exercise with others.

If this is the first time you have encountered the "immunity-to-change language technology," I strongly recommend that you work through the four-column exercise yourself. In working through the four language forms, you will create a mental map of your own built-in resistance to change. If you simply read how it works, you may find it interesting, but you will miss an opportunity to experience the power of this language form in coming to greater awareness of your own inclination not to change. I am a true believer in the wisdom that we cannot ask others to go into places we ourselves are not willing to go. It is in working with our own immune systems that we come to a much better sense of how to help others overcome initial resistance to this process, as well as a better sense of the potential of this exercise to enable change. You will find a blank form for your personal work in Figure 3 at the end of the book.

The four-column exercise is usually presented in a three-hour workshop in which participants are seated in dyads facing the facilitator. If you are presenting this exercise for work on a collective commitment to change, then I suggest participants sit around the same table, so that they may discuss and reflect on the questions together. This exercise is guided by a series of intentionally formulated questions. Participants record their responses in a four-column template. The rhythm of the exercise includes a question from the facilitator, time for personal reflection, sharing in dyads, and then inviting two people to voluntarily offer their responses in the plenary session. To give the participants a model to follow for their own work, the facilitator records the volunteers' responses on the same four-column template on an overhead projector. This same rhythm is followed for each of the four columns. The volunteers are free to withdraw from their public role at any time. If you plan to do this as a collective exercise, give participants an opportunity to do the personal exercise first. This will give them a greater sense of personal engagement in the collective enterprise.

Whenever the "immunity-to-change language technology" is presented, affirm all participants in their sincere commitment to change. A safe, trusting environment is essential, as is the assurance that they can freely choose the depth to which they will engage in this exercise. Because it is difficult to remove our sense of self from the meanings we give to reality, this change process can be threatening to our self-image. Furthermore, because immunity to change is usually perceived as resistance or hypocrisy, it can also make us vulnerable. Make it clear that all of us are a "bundle of contradictions," despite our most sincere commitments.[240] This can help alleviate participants' vulnerability or sense of shame and increase the possibility for greater openness to engage truthfully in the learning exercise. As you become familiar with using this language form, you will come to appreciate your role in supporting and challenging participants according to their particular capacities and potential. In my experience, some prefer to play it safe or engage in the exercise gradually, while others are ready to take the plunge into the depths of their knowing and behaving.

I have chosen three examples to show how these four language forms offer us a structure to reflect on our own praxis and can enable us to surface resistance to change to which we are truly committed. Any of us could be Dorothy or Michael; any of our communities could be the St. Cloud Pastoral Leadership Team. The details are different; however, the natural tendency to carry the simultaneous commitment to change and non-change is the same. Figure 1 gives two examples of how the four-column exercise can be used with individuals. Both Dorothy and Michael are the public players in a pastoral leadership program in which participants meet regularly to reflect on their pastoral praxis. Dorothy is an active member of her parish. She has been affirmed and called by her parish community to take on a leadership role in a variety of ways. Michael is the pastor of a parish community. He truly believes that it is time for the church to say goodbye to "the Club" mentality.[241] Both Dorothy and Michael are committed to moving toward a more inclusive church. As they each work through their individual four-column exercise, it becomes apparent how their immunity to change keeps them from living their commitments.

Figure 2 shows how this same exercise can be used with a group or community as a means to overcome its collective immunity to change. The Pastoral Leadership Team of the St. Cloud Parish comprises eight members of the community, two of whom are ordained and six of whom are lay leaders of various committees. Together, they have worked on implementing practices aimed at developing a deep connection between the community and its leaders in the way they live out their mission as co-disciples. The Pastoral Leadership Team knows that other parish communities are watching to see whether their current community renewal program will be a success. As we move through the team's four-column exercise, we will see how its collective commitment to self-protection keeps the team from fully realizing its commitment to the collective leadership goals the team members espouse. In order to follow through the process, I suggest you begin by covering the columns with a piece of blank paper. Reveal each column one at a time when you are ready to work with it.

Step 1: Shaded column

Filling in the shaded column is the warm-up step, during which participants respond to questions that will help them name their first-column commitment. There are a number of ways to do this step, each of which depends on the context and the goals for using the four-column exercise. One way is to begin by focusing on our common human tendency to complain about what is not working. The "language of complaint" is a very common form of language in many communities. On its own, this way of speaking has very little potential for transformation in that it usually perpetuates a vicious circle of grievances and whining, which can be de-energizing. However, complaints need not be the final word. If we listen to them carefully, we will notice that they often carry within them seeds of our deepest concerns. In this approach, you begin by asking, "If there were things that you could change in your ministry that would make all the difference to your being more effective, what would they be?" Ask participants to write down those complaints in the left-hand shaded column and then to share them with their partner.

Another way of beginning this exercise is to invite participants to brainstorm on what they consider to be important values in ministry and pastoral leadership. Depending on the context, you could open up the conversation for sharing what participants mean when they name certain values and how those values fit into their own vision of church. This is the approach I have used in the examples in figures 1 and 2 in which the participants recorded their own values in the shaded column. When working through this exercise in your own setting, you may find at times that one approach may work better than the other. In both cases, the aim of the work in the shaded column is to lead to the "language of commitment" in column 1.

Figure 1: Four-column exercise (individual work)

	1. Language of Commitment: *I am committed to...*	2. Language of Personal Responsibility: What am I doing/ not doing...
Dorothy - mutuality - clear communication - empathy - dialogue - working with conflict	- dialogue	- I hold back from taking a stance or sharing my convictions in conversations that could clearly benefit from my voice.
Michael - shared leadership - clear vision - mission orientation - listening - interdependence - learning	- interdependence	- When I visit parishioners, I keep my visits very short, having a superficial conversation, giving communion and then leaving after a quick prayer.

Four-column template © Minds at Work

3. Language of Competing Commitment: I am also committed to….	4. Language of Big Assumption I hold: I assume that if… then I….
- I am afraid that I might rock the boat with my opinions or theological viewpoints that are different from what most people around me espouse.	- *I assume that if* I cannot protect myself from the scrutiny of others, *then* I will not be considered as credible. Instead of being credible, I could be considered a troublemaker. This could lead to my being rejected as a member of the pastoral leadership team.
- I am also committed to not saying things that might disturb the status quo; thereby protecting myself from the scrutiny of others	
- I am afraid of not having the right answers to questions they might ask me	- *I assume that* if I do not meet other people's expectations of having all the answers, *then* they will think I am not a good priest. If they do not value me, they may not value priesthood in general or even the church.
- I am also committed to meeting other people's expectations of being an expert on spiritual and religious matters	

Figure 2: Four-column exercise (for collective work)

	1. Language of Commitment *We are committed to...*	2. Language of Personal Responsibility: *What are we doing/ not doing*
St. Cloud Pastoral Leadership Team - mutuality - shared vision - learning - listening - co-discipleship - co-responsibility - clear communication - dialogue - healthy relationships both within community and with diocesan church - purposeful mission	- co-responsibility - co-discipleship	- when some of the parishioners (who we know do not agree with our program) give feedback that challenges some of our practices, *we* tend to ignore it rather than consult with them about how we can all benefit from change

Four-column template © Minds at Work

3. Language of Competing Commitment: **We** *are also committed to....*	**4.** Language of Big Assumption we hold: **We** *assume that if... then we....*
If *we* take those parishioners' feedback about our practices into consideration, we risk not staying on target with our community renewal program.	*We* assume that if *we* do not protect ourselves from confrontation with those who do not agree with us, then we will not meet our target with our community renewal program. Other communities are looking to us and consider our parish to be a model or "light" for the diocese. If we do not meet our target, then we will be considered incompetent or failures. Our failure might send a signal that renewal will never work and others won't even try.
We are also committed to protecting ourselves from confrontation with those who do not agree with how we are going about implementing the community renewal program.	

Column 1: Language of commitment[242]

The language of commitment is designed to transform our complaints into genuine commitments. When we begin by naming our complaints, this language will help us move toward naming our deeper commitments.[243] In attending to the untapped potential of complaints, we can create an environment that honours critical evaluations as opportunities to foster the vitalizing energy of positive commitment.[244] In moving from the unproductive world of complaint, we can encourage people to pursue the transformative potential of their complaints by giving voice to their personal commitments.

As mentioned above, how we speak to ourselves is just as important as how we speak to others. We might find ourselves becoming more and more de-energized because we are incessantly preoccupied with our disappointments or with casting ourselves in a story that is constantly replayed in our heads. On the other hand, we might tell ourselves to ignore or dismiss our complaints. Telling ourselves, "Don't be so negative" or, "Just get on with it" might keep us from accessing the deeper commitments and convictions that are implied in our complaints.

If we begin this exercise in the shaded column with brainstorming of the values we hold for a particular vision of ministry and pastoral leadership, this could be an opportunity to notice the gap between our professed values and what we actually do. In the examples in Figure 1, I had participants take a look at the values they recorded in their shaded column and then asked them, "What is the value to which you are truly committed but not fully realizing?" I went on to say, "When you look at those values, you might find yourself committed to several of them. However, for the purpose of this exercise, choose only one value to which you are truly committed but are not yet *fully* realizing. In other words, choose a value that you are already realizing to some extent, yet, if you were able to live it more fully, your ministry or work or life would flourish even more."

You see in Figure 1 that both Dorothy and Michael chose one value from their lists in the shaded column. Dorothy named dialogue as a value to which she is truly committed but not *fully* realizing; Michael named interdependence. Dorothy's commitment to change is to live more fully the value of dialogue; Michael's commitment to change is to live more fully the value of interdependence. In Figure 2, St. Cloud

Pastoral Team's commitment to change is to live more fully its commitment to co-responsibility as co-disciples.

Column 2: Language of personal responsibility[245]

In this column, we look at our behaviours that are keeping us from *fully* realizing our first-column commitments. I stress the word *fully* because if we are truly committed to a particular value then it is quite likely that we are already doing a lot in support of that first-column commitment. This is the case for the values that Dorothy, Michael, and the St. Cloud Pastoral Team chose; they are ones they are not *fully* realizing. The key question for this column is this: "What are you doing or not doing that undermines you or keeps you from fully realizing your first-column commitment?" The language of this column focuses attention on actions, rather than on disposition, traits, or attitudes.

This column aims to transform our more conventional language of blaming the other into taking responsibility for our actions that work against our first-column commitment. Taking responsibility for our actions does not mean that we must take all the blame or try to fix the system in which we work or minister.[246] There are situations in which others—both individually and collectively—have varying degrees of influence on our behaviours. Furthermore, this language does not deny that some systems and structures of power relations leave people with very little or no choice about how they behave or act. However, this column's emphasis is on the person's capacity to take some (but not all) responsibility for their own actions that work against their sincere commitment to change. And so, a safe and supportive environment is needed for participants not only to tell on themselves but also to call on others to accept their own share of responsibility.[247] The way we respond to this second-column question can allow us to become even more conscious of the larger network of persons and systems that extends beyond the space and time in which we live. And yet, we carry some responsibility for our part in either maintaining the status quo or bringing about change. This awareness is important in ministry in which we could assume all the blame, simply blame the other, or claim powerlessness in the face of outer forces beyond our control. This tendency is evident in Papesh's article, in which he claims that clerics are powerless to say goodbye to the "Club" mentality.[248] The "language of personal responsibility" shows us that we are powerless only to the extent that we are totally unaware of how our behaviours perpetuate the mentality we are committed to changing.

In Figure 1, Dorothy's sincere commitment to dialogue is being undermined by her own behaviours. Using the language of personal responsibility allowed her to see that there are times when she holds back from sharing her convictions and from engaging in dialogue. In Michael's case, although he is committed to interdependence in his faith community, he keeps his pastoral visits brief and superficial, limiting his interactions with people to what are mainly clerical duties, such as giving communion and saying prayers. In the collective example, the St. Cloud Pastoral Leadership Team looked at a familiar pattern in how it receives *and* dismisses feedback from members of its community. The team saw that it pays attention to some of the feedback, especially from those who share similar views on how the parish should develop. The team also saw how it dismisses or ignores the more difficult feedback it receives, especially from those who did not show much support for the team's initiative in the community renewal program. Team members became aware that they have set themselves up for a "them-us" confrontation.

Deep structural change is not possible unless we look at and reflect on our behaviours that contradict or undermine our genuine first-column commitment. Working on the second column enables us to take responsibility for our contradicting behaviours. The fact that we do not practise what we preach is not a new phenomenon. However, it takes courage to name what we are doing—our actual reality—that undermines our true commitment. Usually when we name our contradicting behaviours, we look to focus on either correcting or stopping them completely. However, simply trying to change those behaviours is not a long-term solution, since we have not arrived at their source. New dysfunctional or ineffective behaviours are likely to emerge when we do not address the forces that are at work in us. Even if we make some progress in reducing the second-column behaviours, these forces can hold us in a state of non-change. The second-column work offers the opportunity to stretch and change our ways of thinking as we begin to notice the patterns of our behaviours.

Column 3: Language of competing commitment[249]

This third-column language transforms our more conventional "New Year's resolution" approach to change to an approach that recognizes that we may hold commitments that give rise to the behaviours in column two.[250] Most New Year's resolutions are short-lived, as they do not address deep structural change. Furthermore, because we are often not ready or aware of our need for deep structural change, most of us resume our familiar habits and behaviours by the end of January.

The "language of competing commitment" names a particular form of self-protection to which we are committed. This language is derived from some of the key elements of systems theory that show that all living organisms, humans included, seek to preserve themselves. Closed systems preserve themselves by defending themselves against negative feedback; open systems use that feedback in both their internal and external environments as a sign for change. This language is counter-intuitive, since it uncovers our natural tendency to self-preserve by defending or protecting ourselves from change. The language is designed to surface the incompatibility between our true commitment and what it is we are actually doing. Surfacing and reflecting on the gap between our professed and operative values can be an experience of dissonance.

Dissonance is the psychological tension we experience when our existing beliefs or mindsets are challenged by new insights or behaviours. Our response to dissonance is determined by a complex set of factors, including our personality and history, as well as the event itself. Studies have shown that one of the factors in determining whether dissonance will lead to change is the degree of personal responsibility we take for our actions.[251] The more personal responsibility we take for our contradictory behaviours, the greater the possibility of transformation. Therefore, if an individual or group is truly committed to its first-column values *and* is able to take responsibility for its own second-column behaviours, then it is likely that the amount of dissonance experienced in the top half of this column will be great enough to generate discomfort and motivate the individual or group to alleviate it in some way. How we facilitate the four-column exercise plays an important role in providing a trusting and safe environment for exploring the discomfort and risk of this unknown territory. This is the darkness to which the Gospel of Matthew (6:22-24) refers. If we allow ourselves to move into and begin to bring light into the darkness of our being, we open ourselves to discover rich learnings and resources for more fully realizing our true commitment to change.

The third column is divided in half. To fill in the top half, I ask the following question: "If I were to consider changing those behaviours to better realize the commitment in column one, can I identify anything even vaguely like fear, discomfort, or a sense of loss?" Then I say, "Stay with that feeling of fear, discomfort, or loss for a while and write it in the top half. What you write in the top half will open the way for you to see your hidden immune system. Now move to the bottom half of this third column and ask yourself, "What is my commitment to avoiding this fear, discomfort, or sense of loss?" What you put in this third column should indicate your commitment to self-preservation. One way to assess if you are maximizing this learning opportunity is to ask about the degree of discomfort you have with your findings. Paradoxically, being very uncomfortable with our responses to these questions is considered to be a good sign. The discomfort opens up the possibility for discovering the larger forces that keep us from realizing our commitment. However, the intent of this column is not simply to name the fears we have, but rather to discover that we may be committed to actively avoiding our fears.

As we look at the mental map of the first three columns of Figure 1 for Dorothy and Michael, we notice that the information in the first and third columns is contradictory. Dorothy is committed to dialogue *and* to protecting herself from the scrutiny of others. We can see that her second-column behaviour, which is not voicing her opinion, protects her from scrutiny. Michael is committed to both interdependence *and* to meeting what he considers to be others' expectations that he be an expert in religious and spiritual matters. As he reflects on this reality, he sees that his own self-image is intertwined with those same expectations. His quick visits and superficial conversations protect him from having to face the possibility of questioning or possibly losing his personal and social identity as an expert on religious and spiritual matters. As Figure 2 shows, the Pastoral Leadership Team of St. Cloud Parish is truly committed to co-responsibility and co-discipleship. It is also committed to protecting itself from any negative feedback that might prevent the community renewal program from meeting its target.

The problem is not the competing commitment itself. In fact, competing commitments are normal human motives. The problem is that until we surface our competing commitments, we usually remain unaware of them. By making our competing commitments into objects of our awareness, we recognize that our inner contradictions are a valuable source of challenge and growth. Naming our competing commitments reveals our active, energy-expending way of living that keeps us from fully realizing the first-column commitments. As Figures 1 and 2 show, the third-column language reveals the strength of the dynamic force that maintains the balance between our commitments to change and non-change.[252] The arrows between the first and third columns in the four-column template show that our immune system is made up of countervailing motions that actually keep us in a process of dynamic equilibrium.

Column 4: Language of the big assumption we hold[253]

The fourth language is designed to reveal our hidden big assumption so that we can begin to see and critique it. A big assumption is the mental structure embedded in the competing commitment that keeps us from the change we sincerely intend. The big assumption is usually hidden from our consciousness, yet it holds the power to shape how we understand the world and how we take action. The big assumption is not merely an adequate way of constructing our world, but it is our most adequate construction at that time.[254] This is true for both the individual and the collective psyche. When we look at our big assumption, we move from being subject to it to our big assumption becoming the object of our knowing. As subject, the big assumption is the ultimate principle for shaping our reality and determining our choices and behaviours. When we attend to our big assumption, we become conscious of how it can lead us to systematically notice certain data and to ignore other information.[255] In making the big assumption the object of our knowing, it shifts from being ultimate to becoming relative as we begin to separate our reality from "our way of shaping reality."[256] However, when we begin to look *at* rather than *through* the forms by which we make meaning of reality, "we can be in relation to them"[257] rather than unconsciously subject to them. It would not be an overstatement to say that naming our big assumption can make us very vulnerable, since doing so usually takes us into "highly consequential territory." We begin to see more deeply into ourselves and into the world that we have constructed and in which we live.[258]

Like the third-column language, the "language of the big assumption we hold" is counterintuitive; it also signals change. In working through the fourth column, we first look at our third-column entry and ask, "If I were *not* committed to what is in column 3, then what would that be like for me?" By using an "if... then" phrase, we invert the sentence in the second half of column three. In Figure 1, we see that Dorothy indicated in the third column, "I am also committed to protecting myself from the scrutiny of others." Therefore, her fourth-column entry begins with, "If I do *not* protect myself from the scrutiny of others ...." It concludes with what for her could be the most dire consequences of not realizing the competing commitment named in the third column. Here she adds, "*then* I will not be considered as credible. Instead of being credible, I could be considered a troublemaker. This could lead to my being rejected as a member of the pastoral leadership team." What Dorothy has named as her big assumption has unknowingly set the terms for what she could and could not do within her ministry. Michael's big assumption also flows from his competing commitment. He states, "*I assume that* if I do not meet other people's expectations of having all the answers, *then* they will think I am not a good priest. If they do not value me, they may not value priesthood in general or even the church."

Working with the fourth-column language opened up the space for much discussion among the members of the St. Cloud Pastoral Leadership Team. As Figure 2 shows, the team's big assumption was that "if we do not protect ourselves from confrontation with those who do not agree with us, then we will not meet our target with our community renewal program." While this initial assumption might be true, the group's view of dire consequences of not meeting the target is very telling. The team said, "Other communities are looking to us and consider our parish to be a model or a 'light' for the diocese. If we do not meet our target, then we will be considered incompetent or failures. Our failure might send a signal that renewal will never work and others won't even try."

In all cases, what Dorothy, Michael, and the Pastoral Leadership Team have named as their dire consequences are their most adequate ways of making meaning of their own worlds. These are the assumptions that shape their reality and therefore have a big influence on their actions.

As you see in both Figures 1 and 2, the arrow from the fourth into the third column shows how the big assumption grounds and sustains immune systems. The assumption in column four gives birth to the competing commitment in column three, which in turn generates the personal responsibility noted in column two, which prevents the commitment in column one from being fully realized. What these participants have discovered in completing the fourth column offers them the possibility of unbalancing or leveraging their immune system. By surfacing and identifying the big assumption, they can begin to loosen the hold of unspoken and in some cases unconscious rules that keep their respective and unique immune systems in balance.

The fourth column closes the diagnostic phase of the "immunity-to-change language technology." The follow-up work is another phase with its own set of requirements that enable people to engage in the messy work of observing their big assumptions at work, to seek out their roots, and test the validity of their assumptions. Without it, the diagnostic phase risks being just another opportunity for us to get a glimpse of possibilities for change but then revert to our same behaviours and submerge our new self-awareness below our consciousness.

The Follow-up Phase

The follow-up phase is a time for developing an even greater consciousness of the unique ways in which we resist making the change to which we are truly committed. As we attend to and gradually come to test the validity of our big assumption, we risk decentering our structures of meaning and experiencing disequilibrium. It is for this reason that any follow-up work must be first and foremost supportive for all participants. Depending on the group or individuals with whom we are working, the follow-up work can be offered in a number of ways, either in group or individual sessions. Personal follow-up work can be done individually with a coach, mentor, pastoral supervisor, or spiritual accompanier, or among peers. It can also be done in small groups or seminar-type gatherings. Collective follow-up can take place with a coach or facilitator, who gathers the group on a regular basis. No matter what the design, the follow-up phase as a whole should offer an appropriate balance between support and challenge so that participants can safely examine old, familiar securities that no longer fit with their new experiences and understandings. The follow-up work can also be a space for gaining deeper trust in the process of change itself, opening ourselves to more opportunities for deeper conversion as they arise.

To make this stage a little clearer, we will continue to follow the experience of Dorothy, Michael, and the St. Cloud Pastoral Leadership

Team. Dorothy and Michael were students in pastoral theology and theological field education. Dorothy is also a member of the Centre for Ministry Formation. In their programs, case study presentations in the reflective seminars and the subsequent supervisory and mentoring conversations provide significant learning spaces for first observing how each of their big assumptions hinders effective pastoral practice, particularly in connection with their particular commitments to moving toward a more inclusive church. Their peers helped them notice that while their big assumptions might be true some of the time, they were not necessarily true all of the time. In Dorothy's case, in paying attention to her practice, she discovered that at times when she did share personal convictions that did not always agree with others, her credibility did not suffer. In fact, some people liked the alternative approach she offered. With her mentor, she began to dig up the root of her big assumption, a root that led her back to her early years as a child in an authoritarian family environment. That same environment was reinforced in her experience and the way she made meaning of the power relations in the church. With this new awareness, she was able to see that she could make some choices as to how much power to give to her big assumption. It did not have to determine her destiny. With the support of her peers, she made modest and gradually bolder attempts to share her own truth with others. She came to develop a greater confidence in her ability to share her theological convictions, which were at times quite different from others with whom she ministered. Gradually, in making her meaning system object of her knowing, Dorothy found herself taking on greater responsibility for the choices she made with respect to her place in the group as both co-learner and co-leader.

In Michael's case, his peers and supervisor helped him to notice his discomfort with intimacy and realize that some parishioners might have wanted a more personal conversation during his pastoral visit. He came to see that his own need to have all the answers was deeply ingrained in a well-established cleric–lay model of church in which the cleric has all the answers ready to transmit to the passive world that is waiting for a salvific external intervention. Until he noticed and began to question his big assumption, he was embedded in that same system that kept him from living relations of interdependence to which he was truly committed. In naming his big assumption, he has become more aware of how his behaviours support his simultaneous commitment that continued to uphold a clerical model of ministry. With the support of his supervisor and fellow students, he made significant attempts to have deeper and more personal conversations with others. Gradually, he found himself beginning to pry himself loose from the unspoken expectations that kept him from effective and life-giving pastoral praxis.

With the help of a facilitator, the St. Cloud Pastoral Leadership Team looked at its big assumption, and came to see that it had made its community renewal program into an ideology. In the team's regular meetings, members closely examined their own praxis and began to see that in their dogged convictions for renewal, they had developed a subject-object, top-down mode of leadership that had detached the team from the lived experience and critique of the same community it was committed to serve. They came to see that they themselves were working out of their own exclusionary system of clericalism, in which they had positioned themselves as experts on what the community needed. In gradually opening themselves to the feedback they had until then ignored, they found some of it very helpful for making adjustments to their strategies. But even more important, they came to see that the actual target or end goal was more about the quality of relationships in the community. In making their assumptions object of their knowing—in looking *at* their assumptions, rather than *through* them—Dorothy, Michael, and the St. Cloud Pastoral Leadership Team can begin to take responsibility for and make choices out of what they now know.

In Appendices 1, 2, 3, and 4, you will find some practical suggestions as well as a step-by-step guide for facilitating follow-up work sessions for individual and collective work. When planning your own sessions, keep in mind that just as one language builds on the learnings of the previous language in the diagnostic phase, the follow-up phase is also designed as a sequence of stages aimed at gradually and safely disturbing the inner logic of the big assumption. In other words, do not try to rush and fix the problem too quickly. Like New Year's Resolutions, that approach offers only short-term remedies and superficial change. Allow the follow-up phase to be a space for deep structural change, for enabling our praxis to become more and more authentic.

Conclusion

"If we want deeper understanding of the prospect of change, we must pay closer attention to our own powerful inclinations not to change."[259] The "immunity-to-change language technology" is a tool for attending to those powerful inclinations.. Figures 1 and 2 show that Dorothy, Michael, and the St. Cloud Pastoral Leadership Team are truly committed to more fully realizing values inherent in moving toward a more inclusive church. Yet they are simultaneously committed to protecting themselves from the risks involved in making the changes necessary to fully realize their commitments. At first glance, it may seem odd that all three are truly committed to the very thing that they undermine by engaging in self-protective behaviours that maintain the status quo. This very fact shows how difficult it is to make the deep structural change called for in moving toward a more inclusive church. Change in the way we speak can open the path for change in the way we choose to act.

In his holarchical vision of church, which we discussed in Chapter 5, Wessels tells us that clerics and the laity are free to choose to stop being clerics and laity.[260] However, as we can see, this choice is not as easy as it may seem at first glance. Before we stop behaving in ways that perpetuate the cleric–lay divide, we must first look at and begin to free ourselves from our hidden immune system, which makes us resistant to change. In becoming conscious of our mental structures, through which we make meaning, we can become freer to engage in God's call to the fullness of life. This language offers us much hope for change in the way we interpret reality and choose practices that are life-giving for ourselves and for our church.

Conclusion

In this book, I have invited readers to walk with me through a change process that opens the way for imagining and embracing alternative ways of being church today. This change process is guided by an ecclesial vision of moving toward a more inclusive church in which the Spirit calls *all* of God's people to engage in the development required for our time, incorporating and transforming our rich tradition into innovative ways of living our mission in and for the world. I have argued that clericalism keeps us from fully living out our mission today.

"Clericalism is fundamentally a malady of authority."[261] Despite our most sincere commitment to change, we can all, clergy and laity, suffer from that malady. My own story shows how I act out of tendencies to manage and control in a top-down fashion. When I treat persons as objects, transmitting my pre-packaged truth, withholding information, or using people to satisfy my own needs, I am behaving as a cleric. When I ignore or trivialize painful experiences in my relationship with the church, I collude with the very structures that undermine my own "ecclesiastical dignity and responsibility"[262] and that of others.

In facilitating reflective seminars with students in pastoral leadership, I sometimes use two images to capture the values and theologies that are operative in their pastoral praxis. The first image is a picture of a large head, with a very big mouth, big eyes, very little ears, and a very small body. I was introduced to that image many years ago by José Marins, a Brazilian theologian who enabled the development of many base ecclesial communities in South America and around the world. That image, which he called *Église Grosse Tête* (Church with a Big Head), captures what we mean by the "malady of authority": a big mouth to speak its Truth to the world, and big eyes to make sure that others are conforming, but small ears that don't hear well and a small body that, because of the big head, cannot walk. It must simply sit and remain where and what it is. When we take the time to critically examine our own practice and motives, we might see the Big Head a little more clearly. Sometimes we—individuals, pastoral teams, or the church as a whole—are the Big Head. Sometimes we prefer to have the Big Head in control, so we don't have to take responsibility for our own part in Christ's mission.

The second image is a contemporary painting of the Pentecost, in which all present are touched by the energy and power of the Spirit. The artist, Canada's Gisele Bauche, is well known for the boldness of her colours and forms depicting biblical scenes. The image captures the vibrancy with which the Spirit freely and generously bestows on the whole community the gifts and ministries it needs to fulfill its mission.

Conclusion

I keep copies of these two images back-to-back in a plastic folder so that when students reflect on their praxis, I can easily flip from one image to the other to demonstrate the striking differences in our visions of church and ministry. Together the images capture our simultaneous commitment to change and non-change, a commitment that is natural for all humans. Some situations might trigger a tendency to act more like the Big Head, others to act in the spirit of Pentecost.

As disciples, we continuously seek to enter more fully into relationship with the person of Jesus Christ, whom we believe to be alive and active in our world. Our rich Trinitarian tradition tells us that Jesus is what our own humanity was intended to be: "theonomous, catholic, and in communion, in right relationship, with every creature and with God."[263] As theonomous beings, we are "patterned in relatedness to a relational God for the sake of the world."[264] If I am patterned in relation to an abstract or distant God who is produced and transmitted to me in a subject to object fashion, then it will be difficult for me to realize my vocation clearly articulated in the Second Vatican Council: to become a seeker of "authentic signs of God's presence and purpose" in the world.[265] Our language is a powerful way to pattern our Christian identities and praxis.

A book on language and change would be incomplete without some reference to liturgy. The word *liturgy* is derived from *leitourgia*, a Greek composite word: *leitos* means "people" and *ergo* means "to do."[266] Originally, *leitourgia* referred to a public service undertaken by a citizen to the state. In its biblical usage, *leitourgia* is a service or ministry to the needy, more explicitly the "service or ministry of the priests relative to the prayers and sacrifices offered to God."[267] Over the centuries, we have tended to reduce our understanding of liturgy to the more explicit definition, in which the priests do the work and the laity assists. However, in a critical retrieval of *leitourgia*, assembly for worship and mission for the world are conjoined. Liturgy is the work of the people—*all* subjects—both for the world and God.

The Second Vatican Council sought to correct what had until then become the passive role of the laity in liturgical celebrations by calling all the baptized to "full, conscious, and active participation" in liturgical celebrations.[268] The church considers liturgy to be a privileged place for realizing our vocation to become fully human for the sake of the world. As a consciousness-raising activity, liturgy can and in many cases does contribute to the process of reordering right relationships that engender free and responsible action. In other cases, however, liturgy perpetuates the subject-object, Big Head view of church. The Second Vatican Council's call to consciousness-raising is a call for all the baptized to become active subjects in the life and mission of the church. In this call, the church opened the way for all the baptized to develop as adults in faith. As adults, we take our place as co-disciples, subjects among subjects, seeking to hear and respond to God's presence in the church and world.

Both what we speak and how we speak can either enable or hinder change. Language is one of the resources that can better equip us for living out our Christian mission today. As psychologist Carl Jung maintains, we can either walk upright through the dynamism of life or be "dragged along by fate."[269] There is an intrinsic relationship between developing our consciousness and language, and learning to walk upright as a people of faith today. As human consciousness develops and expands, so too does our "corresponding ability to imagine human possibilities."[270] When we refuse to engage in the meaning-making motion and vitality of life itself, we become victims. On the other hand, when we see through eyes of faith, we can choose to partner with God in the ongoing process of renewal and re-creation. We become freer to "walk

Conclusion

upright" as subjects among subjects, called into fullness of life in the Spirit of the Risen Christ. Language can enable us to walk upright. The language we choose to speak can expand and transform conventional ways of seeing and being church today. Language can help us change the way we read the signs of the times and choose practices that are life-giving for ourselves, for our church, and for the world.

The experiences of Dorothy, Michael, and the St. Cloud Pastoral Leadership Team in both the diagnostic and follow-up phases of the "immunity-to-change language technology" show that change in "how" we speak can help us voice and share our hopes, dreams, and fears. We do not all carry the same hopes, dreams, and fears for the future of our church and mission. If we did, we could be rightly accused of building another Tower of Babel. Yet, unless we bring them to consciousness, reflect on them, and critique them with others who think and feel differently than us, we will continue to be imprisoned by the hidden assumptions and preconceived meanings we impose on reality. In the back and forth between experience and reflection, we open the space for the Spirit to move, and liberation begins to happen. When we bring our hopes, dreams, and fears to the fore, the Spirit is freed and liberation already begins to happen.

As I have said earlier in this book, Christian life is incomplete without imagination. Imagination allows us to dream dreams and see alternate possibilities to what we are living. Some dreams alienate; others liberate and "set in motion an historical work of liberation."[271] However, if someone dreams alone, then it is quite possible it will remain only a dream. In the 1930s, my grandfather's hopes, dreams, and fears remained unspoken. He dreamed dreams alone; his dream of a church defined by human dignity and authentic relations remained a dream.

When many dare to dream together, we open up the possibility of "the beginning of a new reality."[272] In the 1960s, those who gathered for the Second Vatican Council dreamed dreams together of a church called to leave behind its triumphant and exclusive practices and embrace its mission in and for the world. In the 1990s, the quiet conversations at Saint Paul University that led to the opening of the Centre for Ministry Formation allowed me and others to dream dreams together, clearing the way for a new reality of a church in which all the baptized—both lay and ordained—share responsibility for its mission. Dorothy, Michael, and the St. Cloud Pastoral Leadership Team dreamed dreams of a church in which their praxis is marked by dialogue, interdependence, co-responsibility, and co-discipleship. I am grateful for all those who have listened to me voice my hopes, my fears, and my dream into reality. I continue to be strengthened and challenged by friends and colleagues who have chosen to walk with me in sharing my dream for moving toward a more inclusive church with you.

In our ongoing search for meaning in our time and place, we ask many questions about the past. Yet, as "reflective human beings with hopes and dreams in our hearts," it is the future that lures us forward, that inspires and motivates us.[273] As we continue our journey into the fullness of life, we discover the Spirit's call to live with mystery and "develop the wisdom and skill to befriend paradox."[274] Yes, there are ways to befriend the paradox of change and non-change within our praxis as disciples and church. A new language is one of them. And yet, when all we can say has been said, we remain humbly standing in the glory of the One who is Mystery, and there we know that ultimately all is beyond words.

Appendix 1

Facilitating the four-column exercise for individual work

Here are some suggestions and advice for facilitating the four-column exercise with a group of people for *individual work*, including an outline for using the four-column template.

Guidelines

- If you have never facilitated a workshop before, spend some time equipping yourself for this role. I have listed some resources for general facilitation skills at the end of the book. In particular, *How the Way We Talk Can Change the Way We Work*, by Robert Kegan and Lisa Laskow Lahey, will be very helpful. Also, Lahey and Kegan offer practical training for facilitating this exercise through their Minds@Work consulting firm (www.mindsatwork.com).

- Spend some time working with this language form before presenting it to someone else. If participants are to trust the process, they must first trust that the facilitator has worked with it and is capable of leading them safely in this exercise. Don't try to do all this on your own. Invite others to work with this language form individually, and then gather to discuss how it can serve your needs in your context of ministry.

- Keep in mind that each column has its own language in the form of key questions and column headings. While it is important that you explain the intent of each column in your own words, do not change the language of the key questions or the column headings. They are intentionally designed to lead participants to an awareness of their own resistances to change.
- Create a space in which each person is free to participate and work out of their own value system and commitments. Avoid imposing your values on participants.
- Strive to model inclusivity, mutuality, and partnership in your facilitation and language.
- Make time for opening and closing prayer. Be creative and inclusive in your choice of gathering and sending forth prayers, and provide visuals to enhance a prayerful approach to this process. A list of resources for prayer is included at the end of the book.

Set-up

The individual four-column exercise is usually presented in a workshop-style format in which participants are seated two by two facing the facilitator. Arrange tables for two, with enough space for doing written personal work.

Materials needed

- overhead projector
- screen for projection
- markers
- acetate sheet on which the individual blank four-column template has been copied (see Figure 3)
- pens, pencils and blank paper for participants (optional)
- name tags (optional)
- flipchart
- blank four-column exercise sheets for individuals (see Figure 3)
- refreshments for the break

Time

This workshop usually takes 3 hours. Give participants enough time to work through each column at a steady pace but without rushing. Set aside some time at the end to introduce possible steps for the follow-up phase.

Part 1: Introducing the four-column exercise (About 35 minutes)

Step 1: Welcome, introductions and prayer *(10 to 15 minutes)*

Welcome participants, introduce yourself, and share the reason for having this gathering. Invite participants to introduce themselves. Be mindful of the time introductions might take. Ask people to be brief and yet meaningful. I often use the term "M & M" (yes, like the candy) to ask people to use the Minimum of words with the Maximum of meaning when speaking in the group.[275] For example, if people do not know each other, they could give their names, mention their ministry (if applicable), and state a gift that they bring to their community that begins with the same letter as either their first or last name. If the group is over 12 or 15, you could ask them to simply introduce themselves to the persons sitting next to them. You will find other ideas for introductory exercises in the resources for facilitation. Invite participants into prayer.

Step 2: Group discussion *(7 minutes)*

Open a discussion about how participants see or have experienced difficulties in making change with the following or similar questions:

- Have any of you experienced, either in yourself or in others, how hard it is to really change?

- Why do you think change is so hard? Give a few reasons.

Step 3: Response *(5 minutes)*

Respond to their ideas about how difficult change is by affirming what they have said and introducing the concept of immune system. Explain that it is natural for humans to carry a simultaneous commitment to change and non-change.

Step 4: Describe the goal of the exercise *(3 minutes)*

Explain that you will be leading participants through an exercise in which each of them will build a mental map of their own immune systems. They will begin to see how these systems disturb the internal balance that keeps them from making the change to which they are truly committed.

Step 5: Describe the rhythm of the exercise *(3 minutes)*

Tell participants that throughout the exercise you will use the following rhythm: You will first ask a question. They will be given time for personal reflection. Then they will be invited to share in dyads for about 5 minutes. You will ask for two people to offer their responses voluntarily to the group. You will record these responses on a similar four-column template on an overhead projector. This same rhythm will be followed for each of the four columns. Reassure participants that volunteers are free to withdraw from their public role at any time.

Step 6: Hand out the forms *(2 minutes)*

Distribute a blank copy of the four-column template to each participant. (A blank version is found on page 190)

Part 2: The four-column template

(2 hours and 30 minutes, including the short break)

Step 1: Left-hand shaded column *(20 minutes)*

Note: Although there is more than one way to begin the exercise (see Chapter 6), in my experience this one usually works well in groups focusing on pastoral leadership and community renewal.

Invite all participants into a public brainstorming of the values they deem to be important for their ministry. This could be an opportunity to talk about the vision of church and ministry that inspires or challenges them. Then ask them to choose from that list three or four values that are most important to them and record them in the left-hand shaded column. Invite them to share with their partner why those values are significant to them.

Step 2: Column 1 *(20 minutes)*

At the top of Column 1, ask participants to write the words "I am committed to… " Then ask them:

- From the list that you have made in your shaded column, what is the one value that is most important to you at this time?

Acknowledge that all the values they have recorded are likely very important; however, for the purpose of building the mental map, they are to choose only one based on this simple criterion: the value must be important for *them* (not for someone who told them it was important), and they are not fully realizing that value. A good way to check the importance of a value is to ask participants whether it is a 4 or 5 on a scale of 1 to 5 (where 1 is "not very important" and 5 is "very important"). Once they have recorded that value in their first column, invite them to share with their partner what they have written.

Invite two participants to volunteer as public players and to name what they have written in Column 1. Do not discuss why they have chosen those values; simply record them in the first column and thank them for agreeing to be the public players (see Figure 1). Before moving on, check to make sure that all participants can give a 4 or 5 rating to the value they have recorded in Column 1. Draw their attention to the fact that their commitment to change is, in this case, their commitment to live more fully the value that they have named.

Step 3: Column 2 *(20 minutes)*

Affirm participants by acknowledging that because they are so committed to the value they have recorded in Column 1, they are probably doing a lot to realize that value. But because there is room for greater realization, likely something they are doing or not doing is keeping them from living this value as fully as they would like. Invite the participants to write in the top part of Column 2, "What I am doing/not doing…". Then ask:

- What are you doing or not doing that is actually keeping you from fully realizing your first-column commitment?

Ensure that participants focus on concrete actions (or non-actions) or behaviours, not on attitudes or dispositions. (See Figure 1 for examples.) Stress that although others might also have a degree of responsibility for working against their Column 1 commitment, each participant can take some responsibility for the actions he or she has named in Column 2. Some participants could begin to feel ashamed or sheepish about naming behaviours that are contrary to their sincere commitment to change. Reassure them that they are most likely doing a lot to make the change, yet as the following work will show, it is natural to work against those same commitments.

Invite participants to share with their partners what they have written; then ask the public players from Column 1 if they wish to continue. If so, complete Column 2 on the projector and congratulate the public players for their generosity and courage in making their mental maps available to all. If they do not wish to continue, ask for other volunteers.

Refreshment break (20 minutes)

Step 4: ***Column 3*** *(25 minutes)*

Before proceeding to Column 3, first affirm all participants for their honesty in naming their actions and behaviours that work against their first-column commitments. Explain that since most people are aware of their behaviours that work against achieving their goal, such information is not new. However, what *is* new is that they are not going to stop there. Column 3 aims to get at the real issues in the gap between what we profess to be our commitments and what we actually do.

Now draw the participants' attention to Column 3, which is divided into two parts. In the heading section of this column, have them write "I may also be committed to…". Then ask the following question:

- If you imagined yourself not doing what you have written in Column 2, do you have a sense of fear, discomfort, or loss?

Invite them to stay with that feeling and to write it in the top half of the column. (Give them time for personal reflection and to write in the top half of Column 3.)

Explain that their fear or discomfort indicates a commitment that actually competes with their first-column commitment. What is important is not the fear or discomfort itself, but rather the commitment that we, in many cases, unconsciously hold to keeping ourselves away from that fear or discomfort. Ask them to write in the heading of Column 3, "I am also committed to…".

Now ask:

- What is your commitment to overcoming this fear, discomfort, or sense of loss?

What they write in the lower half of this column will indicate their commitment to self-preservation. Offer examples of possible responses (see Figure 1, pages 114–15).

Invite them to share their responses with their partner. Then ask the public players to proceed. If they prefer not to share, ask others if they would volunteer to do so. If no one wishes to share publicly, review the examples from Figure 1 or from your own experience of working with this language form.

Once you have completed Column 3 on the overhead, draw participants' attention to the two arrows on the template encompassing columns 1 to 3. Describe how our built-in immune system keeps us in balance. When we make the change to which we are truly committed in Column 1, our competing commitment kicks in to preserve us by bringing us back to the status quo. Draw participants' attention to their mental map from Column 1 and help them see how their Column 2 behaviours undermine the sincere commitments named in Column 1. Then draw their attention to their mental map from the perspective of Column 3: show them how, in light of their competing commitments (Column 3), their Column 2 behaviours make all the sense in the world. Keep in mind that some participants might feel a sense of shame or hypocrisy about their competing commitments. Affirm them in their very human tendencies to self-protect.

Step 5: Column 4 *(25 minutes)*

Begin this column by explaining the term *big assumptions*. Remind them that big assumptions are our most adequate way of knowing what is real and true for us. Big assumptions set the rules for shaping our reality and determining our choices and behaviours. The problem is not that we have big assumptions, but that they are often hidden from us. Most of us are unconscious of the big assumptions we hold and how they can lead us to systematically pay attention to or ignore certain information, either internal or external. This Column 4 language is designed to surface the big assumptions that are embedded in our competing commitments in Column 3.

Ask participants to write in the heading of Column 4, "I assume that if I am not committed to …, then …". Ask the following question:

- If you were not committed to what you have written in Column 3, what would that mean for you? In other words, what do you believe the consequences for you would be if you did not have your Column 3 commitment?

As you guide participants into these questions, keep in mind that this is where they could be most vulnerable. Their responses could lead them to name some serious consequences that could affect their self-image, desires, and goals, as well as their significant relationships.

Affirm them in their self-honesty and invite them to stay with the big assumption they have named, even if they can immediately rationalize that they don't really believe what they have written. State that even though they don't actually believe it, or at least not all the time, their big assumption likely plays a significant role in holding their immune system in place.

Depending on your context, participants might or might not want to share their big assumptions with a partner or with the group. It is your role as facilitator to gauge how individual participants and the group as a whole are feeling at this point. You might want to offer an example from Figure 1 to help participants get a better grasp of the intent of this column. Even if you do not fill in Column 4 on the template that is shown on the projector, draw participants' attention to the arrow pointing from Column 4 to Column 2.

Explain that now that they have become aware (or more aware) of their big assumption, they have already begun to pry themselves loose from the hold it has on their choices and behaviours. Invite them to reflect on their big assumption. Would it make a big difference to them if they could be freed from it? Have them indicate this point on a scale of 1 to 5, where 1 is "little or no difference" and 5 is "a big difference." If they can give the big assumption a 4 or 5, then they will likely want to engage in the follow-up to this four-column exercise.

Step 6: Bridge between the four-column exercise and follow-up work *(15 minutes)*

Begin by explaining that the follow-up phase is generally helpful for participants once they have done the four-column exercise. This phase will give them opportunities to learn more about the impact of their big assumption on their behaviours. The follow-up phase can be done as personal work, one-on-one conversations with a mentor or

Appendix 1

spiritual director, or as individuals who meet regularly in a group. In all of these ways, there are stages to be followed. Like the four-column exercise, in which each column builds on the other, each stage builds on the other. I suggest that as you present the stages, you write them on a flipchart or print them as handouts for each participant.

Stage 1: Observe the big assumption in action. Invite participants to take the first stage of the follow-up work, which is *not* to change their behaviours but simply to notice what happens or does not happen as a result of their holding their big assumption. Suggest that they journal about what they observe. For many, this step is time to gently befriend their simultaneous commitment to change and non-change and to notice patterns in their behaviours. It might be helpful if you gave them an example from your own experience of this stage or from one of the examples in this book. When Michael (one of the individual participants named in Chapter 6) observed his big assumption in action, he noticed how he felt dissatisfied, short-changed, when he rushed through a visit with a parishioner. He also noticed more and more that some parishioners showed in their body language that they wanted to talk longer with him, but politely said they understood that he was busy and had to leave.

Stage 2: Stay alert to spontaneous experiences that challenge or cast doubt on your big assumptions. In this stage, once again participants are not to change their behaviours, simply pay attention and observe.

Stage 3: Write the biography or story of your big assumption. This is an opportunity to dig around the roots and tell the story of your big assumption and how it was constructed in your own life. In telling and reflecting on our stories, we can gradually loosen ourselves from the unconscious hold of our hidden assumptions.

Stage 4: Design a first test of your big assumption.

Stage 5: Examine the results of your first test

Stage 6: Develop/run/evaluate further tests

Explain that stages 4, 5 and 6 are opportunities to try on some new behaviours and assess the outcomes with the support of this group, if they so desire. Once again, stress the importance of the sequencing of the stages. In other words, you would not suggest that they design tests of the big assumption until they had spent some time observing their big assumptions in action as well as digging up the story. If they move too quickly into the tests, they diminish their opportunity to learn more about the history and impact of what actually keeps them in the state of change and non-change. Also, it would be most helpful to explain to participants that they are free to engage or not engage in this follow-up work. Assure them that if they choose not to continue, that is their choice and it will be fully respected.

If participants choose to meet as a group for the follow-up phase, then propose a time the following month. This will give them time to do their own personal work in Stage 1: that is, observe their big assumption. Appendix 2 provides guidelines for group meetings designed for each of the stages in the follow-up phase.

Close with prayer.

Appendix 2

Facilitating the follow-up phase for individual work in groups

Here is one plan for designing and facilitating the follow-up phase of the "immunity-to-change language technology" for *individual* work in groups. Follow-up work can also be done in a number of one-on-one conversations, such as through mentoring, coaching, or even spiritual accompaniment. There are a variety of ways to facilitate the follow-up phase for individuals in a group. I have chosen to present this particular process as it gives participants time for personal work on each of the stages of the follow-up phase, and allows for open conversation among colleagues or peers. In this section, each of the six sessions is aligned with each stage in the follow-up phase. However, there are times in which Session 1 and Session 2 could be combined so that you would address both stages 1 and 2 in the same session. I have given an example of how you can combine the first two stages in the collective group work in Appendix 4.

Guidelines
- This outline on its own will not make you a skilled facilitator. If you have never facilitated a group before, spend some time equipping yourself for this role. Some resources for facilitation are listed

at the end of the book. In particular, *How the Way We Talk Can Change the Way We Work*, by Robert Kegan and Lisa Laskow Lahey, will be very helpful.

- You should already have done some personal work in the follow-up phase. Otherwise, you risk leading people astray.

- This work is about change; it can make some people feel uncomfortable or vulnerable. It may raise issues for some people that require other forms of personal accompaniment (e.g., therapeutic, spiritual). Be attentive to what participants are sharing and be ready to refer them to other resource persons or professionals.

- The objective of the follow-up phase is to enable people to see and work with their own immune systems in order to make the change to which *they* are truly committed. As in the diagnostic phase, avoid imposing your own values on participants. Create a space in which each person is free to work out of their own value system and commitments.

- Strive to model inclusivity, mutuality, and partnership in your facilitation and language.

- Plan initial activities that help create a safe environment and include all participants. Aim for an environment in which all can work as equals and commit to full participation. If they are to trust the process, they must first trust that the facilitator is capable.

- Make time for opening and closing prayer. Be creative and inclusive in your choice of gathering and sending forth prayers for each session, and provide visuals to enhance a prayerful approach to this process. A list of resources for prayer is included at the end of the book.

Set-up

Create a space in which people are at ease and able to share comfortably with one another. Round tables usually work best for this kind of conversation, because everyone can see each other and make eye contact. If you do not have round tables, set the chairs in a circle and provide some kind of hard surface, such as a clipboard, for participants to write on if they wish.

Materials needed

- flipchart (ideally, one per group for the brainstorming session)
- markers
- blank paper, pens, pencils for participants
- name tags (optional)
- refreshments

Time

Agree on the time you will spend together and stick to it. Each session will require about 1 hour and 30 minutes (2 hours for larger groups). I have not built in a refreshment break. You might want to invite participants to refreshments either before or after the meeting begins. Or, you could adjust the time by including a break within the meeting itself, perhaps between Step 2 and Step 3.

The following sessions for individual work are adapted for a faith context from *How the Way We Talk Can Change the We Work*.

Session 1: Stage 1: Observe the big assumption in action

Step 1: Welcome, prayer, and recap of four-column exercise
(30 minutes)

Begin by offering a brief summary of the diagnostic phase and of immunity-to-change. Depending on your context, you could invite participants to share their experience of doing the four-column exercise. This could also be a time to reopen the question of values, vision, and what people are doing and living with regard to ministry.

Remind participants of the six stages that are part of the follow-up phase. I suggest that you use either the same flipchart paper on which you already wrote the stages, or the handout that you gave at the end of the diagnostic phase (see the closing in Appendix 1). Explain that the follow-up phase is a time in which participants can learn more about themselves and their community, as well as move toward more fully realizing their hopes, values, and vision for ministry. Write your agenda for this session on flipchart paper and explain how you plan to proceed.

Step 2: Sharing observations *(35 minutes)*

As I noted in Step 6 of Appendix 1, you finished the diagnostic phase by inviting participants to begin the first stage in the follow-up work, which is not to change their behaviours but, rather, simply to observe their big assumption in action. Begin this step by asking participants to share what they have noticed about their big assumption since the last time you met. You could recall the story you told at the end of the diagnostic phase of Michael's observations (see end of Appendix 1). Or, if appropriate, you could also disclose elements of your own observations with respect to your big assumption. Depending on the group, you could ask persons to share in dyads before you open up the plenary group discussion. Bring the conversation to closure by connecting the ideas they are discussing to the overall objective of paying attention to and working with our very human built-in resistance to change.

Step 3: Feedback and planning *(10 minutes)*

Ask participants for feedback on this first session. What worked well for them? What would work better in the following sessions? Give them a few minutes of personal time before inviting participants to speak in the plenary. Take the time to affirm the strengths of the gathering and the quality of sharing among participants. Together, plan for any necessary changes for the next meeting. Space your meetings so that everyone has time to personally engage in their follow-up work and not lose the momentum of the group conversation. Some participants might also be meeting with someone one-on-one so, ideally, you will meet once every month or two. Leave this decision to the participants.

Step 4: Preparing for the next stage *(10 minutes)*

Go back to the sheet on which you listed the six stages in the follow-up phase. Invite participants into the next stage by once again asking them *not* to change their behaviours. Instead, ask them to notice any spontaneous experiences that challenge or cast doubt on their big assumption. Suggest that they record in a journal what they notice, and be prepared to report back to the group at the next meeting. To make this clearer, you could give an example from your own experience, or the example of Dorothy's follow-up work in which she noticed that there were times in which she did share her views that were different than others and she was actually accepted by others.

Step 5: Closing

As you move into the closing, ask persons in the group to take responsibility for beginning the next session with a welcome, prayer, and check-in as well as for the closing ritual.

Then move into the closing ritual. There are different ways to close a meeting. You might already have your own. One way could be to ask participants to say just one word that captures a feeling or insight that stays with them as they prepare to leave. I recommend that you close each session with prayer, such as a prayer of thanksgiving, intercessions, or a sending forth prayer.

Session 2: Stage 2: Stay alert to experiences that challenge your big assumption (about 1 hour and 30 minutes)

Step 1: Welcome, prayer and check-in *(20 minutes)*

Offer a brief recap of the last meeting. Invite participants to share their experience of that meeting and their subsequent reflections. Make connections between their sharing, their new awarenesses, and immunity to change. This could be a time to keep exploring how participants are becoming even more aware of their own immunity to change. Write the agenda for this session on flipchart paper and explain how you plan to proceed.

Step 2: Sharing *(50 minutes)*

Invite participants to share their observations about experiences that have cast doubt on their big assumption. Recall the example of Dorothy's experience that was shared at the end of Session 1. If appropriate, you could also share elements of your own experience with this stage. As in the first session, you could ask persons to share in dyads before you open up the plenary group discussion. Explain that they have spent a good part of their lives constructing their big assumptions, which in many cases might be true. But for most, those assumptions they hold are not necessarily true all of the time. Affirm that what they have observed in their own behaviours and actions is normal for most people.

Step 3: Preparing for the next stage (10 minutes)

Go back over the stages of the follow-up phase by referring back to the flipchart paper from the previous session. Affirm the participants in their moving into the stages 1 and 2 and stating that they are not actually leaving those stages behind when they go into Stage 3. Instead, invite them to consider developing a habit of attending to their big assumptions in action; at the same time, suggest they be gentle with themselves. Explain the next stage, in which participants are invited to explore the biography—the story—of their big assumptions. Give them some concrete questions to guide their exploration. For example: When was your big assumption born? How long has it been around? What were some of its critical turning points? If it is appropriate, share a piece of the story of your own exploration, as a model or guide for them. Or, give another example using the Dorothy's or Michael's experience. Again, remind them not to change their behaviours but simply continue to pay attention to how their big assumptions positively or negatively influence their behaviours.

Step 4: Closing (10 minutes)

As you move into the closing, ask participants to take on different roles in the next session. One could offer a brief recap of the session, others the welcome and prayer and check-in. The more people are involved, the greater the opportunity they will have to develop their own sense of belonging to the community. If you choose to design the next session in a similar way to what I have suggested for Session 3, then you will most likely want to take responsibility for the prayer that will bring that conversation to closure. Then move into the closing ritual. You could use the same process described in Session 1, in which participants share one word that captures a feeling or insight that stays with them as they prepare to leave. You could also close with a prayer in which participants name one gift they have received during that session for which they are grateful.

APPENDIX 2

Session 3: Stage 3: Reflect on the biography of your big assumption (1 hour and 30 minutes)

Step 1: Welcome, prayer, and check-in (15 minutes)

Ideally, participants will have taken responsibility for welcoming as well as leading opening prayer and some form of check-in. The check-in could be simply inviting people to share something they are celebrating at this time. After either you or a participant has offered a brief summary of the last session, invite participants to share their experience of that meeting and their subsequent reflections. This is another opportunity to make connections between their experience and their sincere commitments to change. Write your agenda for the session on flipchart paper and explain how you plan to proceed.

Step 2: Sharing (60 minutes)

This step calls for a careful reading of the group in discerning how to proceed. Some groups are small and close relationships have been formed. Other groups might tend to limit the depth of their sharing. In all cases, let the group, as well as each participant, determine the breadth and depth of their self-disclosure. Come to some kind of consensus around what sharing the group is comfortable with. Ask the group how best to proceed, given the time allotted to this session. How many people speak and how much time each person has to share depends on the size of the group. Decide this in advance so that no one feels rushed or left out. If necessary, have half the group speak during this session and the rest speak at the next one (you could design it in a similar fashion, before proceeding to the next stage of the follow-up phase). Ask the group how they would like this sharing facilitated. For some groups, a talking stick or similar object can be used as a way to ensure the speaker has everyone's full attention.

Some participants might prefer to share what they have learned in reflecting on the story of their big assumptions; others might want to share the stories themselves. Before anyone speaks, ask the group to honour each person by listening attentively, without judgment. Begin the conversation by asking a general question: What have you discovered as you explored the history of your big assumption? After each person has finished speaking, invite the group to be silent for a few minutes, then invite feedback. As a way to respect the integrity of the person's story and the relationships in the group, you might find it helpful to guide the feedback session with a question such as this: What has touched you in (name)'s story?

Step 3: Closing the conversation with prayer (15 minutes)

Once all participants have shared, close the conversation with a time of silence followed by a gesture of gratitude for the richness of the discussion. This could be a spontaneous prayer or a litany of thanksgiving prepared in advance.

Step 4: Preparing for the next stage (5 minutes)

If all participants have finished sharing their stories, invite participants to continue reflecting on the history of their big assumption. Again, remind them not to change their behaviours but simply continue to pay attention to how their big assumption affects their behaviours. In preparation for the next stage, invite them to consider what kind of modest test they might design as a safe test for their big assumptions. Ask for participants to take responsibility for opening and closing the next session.

Session 4: Stage 4: Design a first test of your big assumption

(1 hour and 30 minutes)

Step 1: Welcome, prayer and check-in (15 minutes)

As with the previous sessions, participants who agreed to take responsibility for this step will welcome, lead the prayer and do check-in. If a participant is summarizing the last meeting, invite other comments on the experience of the last session. If appropriate, make connections between participants' experience and your experience of the power of story as it is told and reflected upon in community.

Step 2: Sharing (60 minutes)

Begin with a discussion of how big assumptions are embedded in our competing commitments. (It might be helpful to use the examples in Figure 1, pages 114–15). Ask them to look at their own four-column exercise. Refer to the two arrows between Columns 1 and 3 that show how our competing commitments keep us in a state of equilibrium, of simultaneous change and non-change. Then bring their attention to the arrow that extends from the fourth column right into the second column. This is how I suggest you explain this: In the fourth column of the diagnostic phase, we moved from being subject to the big assumption to the big assumption becoming object of knowing. Then, in the first three stages of the follow-up phase, in observing it in action and digging up its roots—its biography—we began to disturb its inner logic. Already, our growing awareness makes us a little freer of its hold on us. In this stage of the follow-up phase, you are going use this arrow between Column 4 and 2 as a lever to go even further in freeing yourself from your big assumption. In this stage, you will design a modest and safe test to your big assumption.

It might be helpful to elaborate on Dorothy's follow-up phase to demonstrate possibilities. Dorothy was preparing to attend the next parish council meeting, where one item to be discussed was whether to offer financial support to an ecumenical chaplain in the neighbouring low-income community. Dorothy knew that most of the council did not favour that proposal. Many had already grumbled about it after Sunday Eucharist, saying, "Why would those people not just come to see us here at church if they need help? Father is here to help them. Why should we pay someone—a layperson at that—to do ministry outside the church itself?" When Dorothy heard those comments in the parking lot, she bristled and said nothing. Yet, she felt strongly that the church's mission was about meeting people where they lived, right in the community. She was deeply inspired by how Jesus had chosen to minister right in the midst of people's lives. In preparation for the meeting, she designed a test to her big assumption. She wanted to see how she might be regarded by the other members of council if she voiced her conviction.

After sharing this example, invite participants to share questions and concerns before trying their own design. Depending on the size of the group, participants could do this work in dyads and then share in the larger group what they have planned. Ask them to name the signs they will look for in testing the validity of their big assumption. If they did work with a partner in this session, you could suggest that they check in with their partner before the next session to talk about how their tests are going.

Before closing, ask participants to take responsibility for opening and closing the next session.

Step 3: Closing ritual and prayer

Because of the nature of this stage, you could close this session by asking participants to name what they need (e.g., courage, strength, boldness, humility) to go ahead with the test they have designed. The closing prayer could be a time for offering all these needs in some form of intercessory prayer.

Session 5: Stage 5: Examine the results of your first test

(1 hour and 30 minutes)

Step 1: Welcome, prayer, and check-in (15 minutes)

The persons who offered to take responsibility for opening the session welcome, lead the prayer, do check-in, and offer a recap of the last session. Invite participants to voice further reflections on that session.

Step 2: Sharing (60 minutes)

Open the space for sharing and examining the results of their first tests. As when they shared the history of their big assumption, the group will determine the extent of the sharing. Write the following or similar questions on a flipchart as a way to guide the conversation:

- What do the results of your test tell you about the validity of your big assumption?
- Is your big assumption more accurate with some people or in some situations than in others?
- Why is that the case?

Give participants about 5 minutes of personal time, then ask them to share with the same partner with whom they designed the test. Then open the conversation in the plenary. Remind the group that as with all sharing, this is a time for receiving each story with openness and reverence. Give each person the space to share according to the time allotted, then spend a few moments in silence. Provide encouragement and feedback that will build and support each person in his or her commitment to change.

Step 3: Preparing for the next stage *(10 minutes)*

Refer back to the flipchart, on which you wrote the six stages in the follow-up phase. Open up a brief conversation to get a sense of where participants are at in their own change process. Explain that the next stage is an opportunity to develop, run, and evaluate further tests so that they can work at leveraging even more the inner logic of the big assumption that keeps them from making the change to which they are truly committed. In this next stage, participants might prefer to work more closely with a partner and schedule their next group meeting in a few months. That would give them more time to do further testing. As well as working with a partner, they might also find the support of the whole group very helpful and prefer to keep meeting monthly or bimonthly. Leave this decision to the group; prepare for the next session in a way that supports that choice.

Step 4: Closing ritual and sending forth prayer *(5 minutes)*

You could close in ways that are similar to other sessions, inviting participants to simply share how they leave the session. If the group has decided to work with a partner in between meetings, then the closing prayer could be inspired by Jesus' sending forth his disciples two by two.

Session 6: Stage 6: Develop, run, and evaluate further tests

Participants left Session 5 with an invitation to design and run further tests, most probably with a partner. I suggest that you design Session 6 and any subsequent sessions similar to Session 5, beginning with the opening step, into the next step with sharing the results and designing new tests. It is quite possible that by this time, the group will have achieved its goal of providing a space for individuals to work through their own resistance to change. However, the group can continue to meet, taking its own learning and faith formation further.

Appendix 3

Facilitating the four-column exercise for group work

Here are some suggestions for facilitating the four-column exercise for *collective* work, including an outline for using the four-column template. Before using this language form as a collective exercise, all participants should have first had an opportunity to do the individual work. This will give them a greater sense of personal engagement and responsibility in the collective enterprise.

Guidelines

- If you have never facilitated a workshop before, spend some time equipping yourself for this role. I have listed some resources for general facilitation skills at the end of the book. In particular, *How the Way We Talk Can Change the Way We Work*, by Robert Kegan and Lisa Laskow Lahey, will be very helpful. Also, Lahey and Kegan offer practical training for facilitating this exercise through their Minds@Work consulting firm (www.mindsatwork. com <http://www.mindsatwork.com/>).

- Spend some time working with this language form before presenting it to someone else. If participants are to trust the process, they must first trust that the facilitator has worked with it and is capable of leading them safely in this exercise. Don't try to do all this on your own. Invite others to work with this language form individu-

ally, and then gather to discuss how it can serve your needs in your context of ministry.
- Do collective work only after participants have done the work individually. Ideally, they will have also had the opportunity to do some follow-up work (see Appendix 2). If you are not able to gather all participants at the same time for individual work, meet with them one on one.
- Strive to model inclusivity, mutuality, and partnership in your facilitation and language.
- Create a space in which each person is free to participate and work out of his or her own value system and commitments. Avoid imposing your values on participants.
- Make time for opening and closing prayer. Be creative and inclusive in your choice of gathering and sending forth prayers, and provide visuals to enhance a prayerful approach to this process. A list of resources for prayer is included at the end of the book.

Set-up

The four-column exercise is usually presented in a workshop-style format in which participants can easily move their chairs to see the facilitator and be comfortably seated around tables for discussion with their group. Ideally, the groups will be no larger than 12 people so everyone can contribute. If you are just beginning this kind of facilitation, you might want to consider having only one or two groups at a time with no more than eight per group. As you become more familiar with the process, the goals and needs of the community will help you determine the right number of groups to facilitate in the same session.

Materials needed

- overhead projector
- screen for projection
- markers
- acetate sheet on which the collective blank four-column template has been copied (see Figure 4)
- pens, pencils and blank paper for participants (optional)

- name tags (optional)
- flipchart
- blank collective four-column exercise sheets (one for each participant and one more for the whole group – see Figure 4)
- refreshments for the break

Time

As with the workshop for individuals, this collective one should also take about 3 hours. However, be flexible. If you have more than eight participants per group, consider planning for more time. For example, if you have one or more groups of 12, you could offer a full-day session: 3 hours in the morning, a 1-hour break for lunch, and 2 hours in the afternoon. The reason I suggest a longer time for a larger group is that each group needs an adequate amount of time to work through each of the four columns at a steady pace with opportunities for good discussion. In planning your overall time, be sure to set aside some time at the end of the workshop to introduce possible steps for the follow-up phase. The times I have indicated below are for a 3-hour meeting with two groups of eight people.

Part 1: Introducing the four-column exercise (35 minutes)

Step 1: *Welcome, introductions, and prayer* (15 minutes)

Welcome participants and state the reason for this gathering. Since each group has accepted the invitation to do collective work, it would be right to assume that the participants in each group know each other. Because each participant in the group will be asked to engage in fairly intense discussion during the four column exercise, it is often helpful to begin the workshop with some type of inclusion or trust-building exercise. For instance, to build interpersonal trust, you could invite participants to share with members of their group one piece of personal information, such as something they are very passionate about. (You will find other suggestions for these types of opening exercises in the resources for facilitators at the end of the book.) Bring this step to closure by inviting participants into prayer.

Step 2: Opening discussion *(15 minutes)*

Invite participants to describe briefly their experience of the individual work and their ongoing hopes and commitment for working toward change or renewal in their communities. Invite people to share using what I have described in Appendix 1 as the M & M principle: Minimum of words with the Maximum of meaning.

Use the sharing as an opportunity to recall the discussion from individual work about how participants see or have had difficulties in making change. Why is change so difficult? Remind them of the concept of our built-in immune system. As they learned in the previous workshop, it is natural for humans, individually and collectively, to carry a simultaneous commitment to change and non-change. Like individuals, groups or organizations also hold big assumptions that anchor their simultaneous commitments to change and non-change.

Step 3: Describe the goal of the exercise *(4 minutes)*

Explain that you will be leading groups through an exercise in which together they will build a mental map of their own collective immune system. Explain that even though they have done individual work, the group as a whole has its own collective immune system that may or may not resemble the members' individual ones. As with the individual work, as people work through the exercise, they will begin to see how their collective immune system maintains the internal balance that keeps them from making the change to which they are truly committed.

Step 4: Describe the rhythm of the exercise *(4 minutes)*

Explain that you will follow a rhythm similar to that of the individual diagnostic phase. The rhythm goes like this: you will ask a question. They will then be given time for personal reflection before moving into their group dialogue. Stress the understanding that all members of the group share responsibility for the quality of their conversation and work. Ask each group to call forth a facilitator as well as at least one recorder. The facilitator will serve the group by actively monitoring the space so that all voices can be heard without judgment. The recorder will use the flipchart in the brainstorming session and as required to help guide the group dialogue. Another (or the same) recorder will fill in the final collective four-column exercise on behalf of the whole group. Invite both groups to be public players (as in the individual exercise). If one or both agree, then you will record these responses on the acetate four-column template on the overhead projector. Reassure participants that the volunteers are free to withdraw from their public role at any time. This reassurance might free the group to share at a deeper level. If they prefer not to be public players, you could use the St. Cloud Pastoral Team entries in Figure 2 (Chapter 6) to guide them through the process. The same rhythm will be followed for each of the four columns. As with the individual diagnostic phase, be sure to use the same questions given below in each of the four columns.

Step 5: Hand out the forms *(2 minutes)*

Distribute a blank copy of the collective four-column template to each member of the group for their own personal work, as well as one that the recorder will use to write down the group's responses. It might also be helpful to have blank paper and pencils or pens for participants to make their own notes as they proceed through the exercise.

Part 2: The four-column template (2 hours and 25 minutes)

Step 1: Left-hand shaded column *(15 minutes)*

Note: Although there is more than one way to begin the exercise (see Chapter 6), the one I offer here works well for pastoral leadership development and community renewal.

Invite each group into its own brainstorming of the values they deem to be important for their particular ministry and mission as a group. Ask the recorder to write all of the values on a flipchart so that everyone can see what is written in the shaded column. Invite participants to share among themselves why those values are significant to them. This could be an opportunity to make connections between the values they have named and the vision of church, mission, and ministry that inspires or challenges them.

Step 2: Column 1 *(15 minutes)*

At the top of Column 1, ask the group recorder to write the words "We are committed to…". Then ask:

- From the list that you have made on the flipchart, what is the one (or, at the most, two) value that is most important to you as a group at this time?

Invite them into a group discussion. This work assumes that the participants are able to listen to each other and are prepared to come to some consensus as to the most important values for the group, not simply for them as individuals. If they do choose two values, ask them, for the purpose of this exercise, to make sure that they are complementary and not opposed to one another. Otherwise, their mental map will serve little use in unearthing their simultaneous commitments to change and non-change. Use the example of the St. Cloud Parish Leadership Team to clarify what you mean by complementary values (e.g., co-responsibility and co-discipleship). Acknowledge that the values they have recorded are likely very important; however, for the purpose of building the mental map, they are to choose only two, based on some simple criteria: first, the values must be important for *them* (not for someone who told them these values were important), and second, they are not fully realizing these values.

A good way to check the importance of a value is to ask participants whether, as a group, it is a 4 or 5 on a scale of 1 to 5 (where 1 is "not very important" and 5 is "very important"). Invite a spokesperson on behalf of each group to be public players and to name what their groups have written in Column 1. Do not discuss why they have chosen those values; simply record them and thank them for agreeing to be the public players. Before moving on, check to make sure that all groups can give a 4 or 5 rating to the value they have recorded in Column 1. This is also the time to note that each group's commitment to change is, in this case, their commitment to live more fully the value that they have named.

Step 3: Column 2 *(25 minutes)*

Affirm each group by acknowledging that because they are so committed to the value they have recorded in Column 1, they are probably doing a lot to realize that value. But because there is room for greater realization, likely something they are doing or not doing is keeping them from living this value as fully as they would like.

Invite the group recorder to write in the top part of Column 2, "What we are doing/not doing…". Then ask the following question:

- What are you (as a group) doing or not doing that is actually keeping your group from fully realizing your first-column commitment?

Invite the participants into a 3-minute personal time for reflecting on this question. Then invite them into a group dialogue about what each participant has noted. It might be helpful for the recorder to make notes on the flipchart. Ensure that the discussion focuses on concrete actions or behaviours, not on attitudes or dispositions. Invite the group to look at how the behaviours or actions work against their first-column commitments. Encourage them to be concrete and share what they have experienced and observed. Also, stress that although others might also have a degree of responsibility for working against the group's Column 1 commitment, each group can take some responsibility for the actions named in Column 2. Some groups could begin to feel ashamed or sheepish about naming behaviours that are contrary to their sincere commitment to change. Reassure them that they are most likely doing a lot to make the change, yet, as the following work will show, it is natural to work against those same commitments. Remind them that what they encountered as similar tendencies in doing their individual work is also true for groups. The objective is to come to some understanding and consensus as to what they are doing or not doing as a group that is undermining their first-column commitment.

Ask the public players for Column 1 if they wish to continue. If so, complete Column 2 on the projector and thank them for their generosity in making their groups' mental maps available to all. If the first two public players do not wish to share, use the example from Figure 2.

Refreshment break (15 minutes)

Step 4: Column 3 *(30 minutes)*

Affirm the groups for their courage in being honest with themselves in Column 2. Since most people are aware of their behaviours that work against achieving their goals, such information is not new. What *is* new is that they are not going to stop there. Column 3 aims to get at the real issues in the gap between what we profess to be our commitments and what we actually do.

Now point the groups to Column 3, which is already divided into two parts. In the heading section of this column, have them write, "We may also be committed to...". Then pose the following question:

- If you imagined yourselves as a group not doing what you have written in Column 2, do you have a sense of fear, discomfort, or loss?

Invite them to stay with that feeling and to write it in the top half of the column. Give about 3 or 4 minutes for personal reflection and then proceed to a group discussion.

Now ask:

- What is your collective commitment to avoiding this fear, discomfort, or sense of loss?

Again, give a few minutes of personal time before entering into the group discussion. What they write in the lower half of this column will indicate their commitment to self-preservation. Offer an example of possible responses (see Figure 2, pages 116–17). Some groups might need a fair amount of time to work through this column. Make yourself available to coach them along. Then invite the public players to proceed. If they prefer not to share, ask others to do so. If no one wishes to share publicly, review examples from Figure 2 or from your own experience of working with this language form with other groups.

Once you have completed Column 3 on the overhead, draw participants' attention to the two arrows encompassing columns 1 to 3 on the template. Describe how our built-in immune system keeps us in balance. When we make the change to which we are truly committed in Column 1, our competing commitment kicks in to preserve us from the discomfort of change by bringing us back to the status quo. Draw the groups' attention to their mental map from the perspective of Column 1, helping them see how their Column 2 behaviours undermine the sincere commitment named in Column 1. Then draw their attention to their mental map from the perspective of Column 3: show them how, in light of their competing commitments, their Column 2 behaviours make all the sense in the world. Keep in mind that some groups might feel a sense of shame or hypocrisy about their competing commitments. Affirm them, both individually and collectively, in their very human tendencies to self-protect.

Step 5: Column 4 *(30 minutes)*

Begin this column by recalling what they had encountered and understood by the term *big assumptions* in their individual work. Remind participants that big assumptions are our most adequate way of knowing what is real and true for us. Big assumptions set the rules for shaping our reality and determining our choices and behaviours. The problem is not that we have big assumptions, but that they are often hidden from us, both individually and collectively. Most of us are unconscious of the big assumptions we hold and how they can lead us to systematically pay attention to or ignore certain information, either internal or external. The Column 4 language is designed to surface the big assumptions that are embedded in competing commitments in Column 3.

Ask the groups to write in the heading of Column 4, "We assume that if we are not committed to ..., then ... ". Present the following question:

- If you as a group were not committed to what you have written in Column 3, what would that mean for you? In other words, what do you believe the consequences would be for your group if you did not have your Column 3 commitment?

As you guide the groups into these questions, keep in mind that this is where they could be most vulnerable. Their responses could lead them to name some serious consequences that affect their self-image, desires, and goals, as well as their significant relationships.

Affirm them in their self-honesty and invite them to stay with the big assumption they have named, even if they can immediately rationalize that they don't really believe what they have written. State that even though they don't actually believe it, or at least not all the time, their big assumption likely plays a significant role in anchoring their immune systems.

As with the other columns, give participants some personal time for reflection before proceeding to a group discussion. Depending on your context, the groups might or might not want to share their big assumption in the public forum. It is your role as facilitator to gauge how they are feeling at this point. You could offer an example from Figure 2 to help groups get a better grasp of the intent of this column. Even if you do not fill in Column 4 on the template that is shown on the overhead, draw participants' attention to the arrow pointing from Column 4 to Column 2.

Explain that now that they have become aware (or more aware) of their big assumption, they have already begun to pry themselves loose from the hold it has on their choices and behaviours. Invite them to reflect on their big assumptions. Ask:

- Would it make a big difference to you if you could be freed from your big assumptions?

Have them indicate this point on a scale of 1 to 5, where 1 is "little or no difference" and 5 is "a big difference." If they can give the big assumption a 4 or 5, then they will likely want to engage in the follow-up to this four-column exercise.

Step 6: Bridge between the diagnostic phase and the follow-up phase

Explain in general terms what the follow-up phase entails. Remind them of the six stages that are the same for individual work. Write those stages on a flipchart for easy reference.

Stage 1: Observe the big assumption in action. If they choose to go into the follow-up phase, this will be their first task. Do not change any behaviours or actions. Simply observe what is going on.

Stage 2: Stay alert to any spontaneous experiences that challenge or cast doubt on their big assumption. This will be their second task. Once again, participants will be asked *not* to change their behaviours. They are simply to pay attention and observe. Suggest that in the follow-up phase, they could put stages 1 and 2 together. They might find it helpful to record what they notice in a journal and discuss it further when they meet. If they did individual follow-up work, you could refer back to their personal experience. If not, you could use the St. Cloud Pastoral Leadership Team as an example. In the first two stages of their follow-up work, they noticed that when their big assumption (see Figure 2, pages 116–17) was in action, even though the team was not receiving the "negative" feedback, it was actually draining the energy and enthusiasm for the renewal program in the parish. They also noticed that there were times when the "negative" feedback was actually helping them stay on track. For instance, the feedback helped them to see that they were moving too quickly without giving parishioners enough time and information so that they could understand the changes being proposed.

Stage 3: As with the individual work, you will have an opportunity to search out the biography or story of your big assumption.

Stage 4: Design a first test of your big assumption.

Stage 5: Examine the results of your first test.

Stage 6: Develop/run/evaluate further tests.

Explain that steps 4, 5, and 6 are opportunities to try on some new behaviours and assess the outcomes with the support of this group, if they so desire. Stress the importance of the sequencing of the steps. In other words, you would not suggest that they design tests of the big assumption until they had spent some time observing their big assumptions in action as well as digging up the story. If we move too quickly into simply trying to change our behaviours, we diminish our opportunity to learn more about the history and impact of what actually keeps us in the state of change and non-change.

Suggest that follow-up work can be done by the group itself or with an outside facilitator or coach. Also, suggest that it would be best that only one group meet at a time. In other words, if more than one group met to do the diagnostic phase together, it would probably be more helpful for the groups to meet separately. Finally, assure them that they are free to choose whether to engage in follow-up work at all. They will be respected in their decision. If they do not choose to do follow-up, thank them for coming and express your hope that this exercise has been helpful for them in their own desire to realize their commitments.

If they do choose to do some kind of follow-up work, finish by inviting groups to take the first and second steps of follow-up work in which they are *not* to change their behaviours, but simply to observe their big assumption in action and stay alert to any spontaneous experiences that challenge or cast doubt on their big assumptions. Suggest that they journal about what they observe and report back to each other at their next regular meeting. Invite the group(s) to gather again, ideally in one month, to discuss what they have observed, either together or in small groups. At that time, you may invite them to design together a follow-up session. See Appendix 4 for some suggestions for designing a follow-up phase for collective work.

Close with prayer.

Appendix 4

Facilitating the collective follow-up phase

Here is one plan for designing and facilitating the collective follow-up phase of the "immunity-to-change language technology." Note that the collective follow-up phase group work can be done either by the group itself as part of its regular meetings (e.g., monthly pastoral leadership meetings) or in sessions that are designed and facilitated by someone who is not part of the group itself (e.g., facilitator or coach). This model is facilitated by an outside facilitator for meetings focused only on the follow-up work. It is a variation of the individual follow-up phase in which I have combined stages 1 and 2 of the follow-up phase in the first session.

Guidelines

- If you have never facilitated a group process before, spend some time equipping yourself for this role. Some resources for facilitation are listed at the end of the book. In particular, *How the Way We Talk Can Change the Way We Work*, by Robert Kegan and Lisa Laskow Lahey, will be very helpful.

- You should already have done your own individual follow-up work. Otherwise, you risk leading people astray.

- The objective of this exercise is to enable people to see and work with their own immune systems in order to make the change to which *they* are truly committed. As in the diagnostic phase, avoid imposing your own values on participants. Create a space in which each person is free to work out of their own personal value system and commitments.

- This work can make some people feel uneasy. It can also cause some conflict within the group itself. Ensure that you or your colleagues are equipped to enable a group to work with its conflict. This could be fertile ground for new awarenesses and development.
- Strive to model inclusivity, mutuality, and partnership in your facilitation and language.
- Plan initial activities that help create a safe environment and include all participants.
- Aim for an environment in which all can work as equals and commit to full participation.
- Make time for opening and closing prayer for each session. Be creative and inclusive in your choice of gathering and sending forth prayers, and provide visuals to enhance a prayerful approach to this process. A list of resources for prayer is included at the end of the book.

Set-up

Create a space in which people are at ease and able to share comfortably with one another. Circles usually work best for this kind of conversation, because everyone can see each other and make eye contact. If you do not have round tables, make some kind of hard surface, such as clipboards, available for participants to write on if they wish.

Materials needed

- flipchart
- markers
- blank paper, pens, pencils for participants
- refreshments

Time

Agree on the time you will spend together and stick to it. Each session will require about 2 hours. Ideally, groups will not exceed 12 participants.

The following sessions are one suggestion for collective work in faith-based groups that has been adapted from the individual follow-up phase found in *How the Way We Talk Can Change the Way We Work*.

Session 1: Stages 1 and 2 of the follow-up phase

1. Observe the big assumption in action, and

2. Stay alert to any spontaneous experiences that challenge or cast doubt on their big assumption.

Step 1: Welcome, prayer, and recap of the four-column exercise (40 minutes)

Begin with a brief summary of the diagnostic phase and of immunity-to-change. Invite participants to review and share their experience of doing the four-column exercise as a group. Present this phase as a time in which they may become clearer about their hopes, dreams, and fears in their attempts to more fully realize their commitments in leadership and ministry. Keep in mind that you are accompanying them in developing the habit of reflecting on their praxis, in order that they see more clearly the values and vision that are embedded in their behaviours and actions.

Refer to the flipchart on which you recorded the six stages of the follow-up phase and remind them that in this session you will work with the first two stages. Remind them that at the end of the four-column exercise (see Appendix 3), you asked them to do two things: first, not to change their behaviours but rather, simply to observe their big assumption in action; and second, to be attentive to any spontaneous experiences that challenge or cast doubt on their big assumption.

Step 2: Sharing their observations of their big assumption in action, as well as the experiences that have challenged or cast doubt on their big assumption (50 minutes)

Invite them also to share what they noticed in observing their big assumption in action. Then invite them to share their observations about any experiences that have cast doubt on their big assumptions. Encourage them to give concrete examples and to freely discuss the impact of those observations on their big assumption. Depending on the group dynamic, you could begin this step by first asking participants to share in dyads and then in the larger group. Or, it might be more helpful to begin the conversation within the group as a whole. Bring the conversation to closure by connecting their experience and insights to the overall objective of paying attention to and working with our built-in resistance to change. As with the individual work, explain that this kind of growing awareness is giving them more leverage in freeing themselves as a group from what until recently were their unconscious assumptions (refer to the arrow that extends from Column 4 to Column 2 in Figure 4).

Step 3: Feedback and planning (15 minutes)

Ask participants for feedback on their experience of this session. What worked well for them? What might be more helpful in the following sessions? Together, plan for any necessary changes for the next meeting. Space your meetings so that the group has time to engage in its follow-up work and not lose the momentum of the follow-up conversation. Leave this decision to the participants.

Step 4: Preparing for the next stage (15 minutes)

Explain the next stage, in which participants are invited to explore the history of their big assumptions. Give them some concrete questions to guide their exploration. For example:

- When was your big assumption born?
- How long has it been around?
- What were some of its critical turning points?

Explain that their big assumptions not only emerge out of their personal histories, but are also in the development of their faith community and institution in which they are ministering. In other words, we are well formed in our own faith tradition and have unconsciously assimilated assumptions about our roles and expectations that affect our choices. Depending on your context, you could ask them to reflect on the development of their own group and its place within the structure and life of the larger community. Again, remind them not to change their behaviours but simply continue to pay attention to how their big assumptions positively or negatively influence their behaviours. Before closing, ask a few people to take responsibility for beginning the next session with a welcome, prayer, and check-in.

Step 5: Closing ritual and sending forth prayer

See Appendix 2 and prayer resources for suggestions.

Session 2: Stage 3: Reflect on the history of your big assumption

Step 1: Welcome, prayer, and check-in (15 minutes)

Participants who offered to take responsibility for leading this session lead the prayer, do check-in, and offer a brief recap of the last session. Invite participants to share their experience of that meeting and their subsequent reflections.

Step 2: Sharing the history of your big assumption (80 minutes)

Invite participants to speak about what they have discovered as they explored the history of their big assumption. Before anyone speaks, ask people to honour each story by listening attentively, without judgment. Ask the group how best to proceed, given the time allotted to the session. How much time each person has to share depends on the size of the group. Decide this in advance so that no one feels rushed or left out. Ask the group how they would like this sharing facilitated. For some groups, a talking stick or similar object can be used as a way for the speaker to receive full attention.

You could begin the conversation by asking a general question: What have you discovered as you explored the history of your group's big assumption? You or another person could record key elements of the conversation on a flipchart. Depending on the number of elements being recorded, you could facilitate a process that helps the group chart the big assumption's historical development from a number of viewpoints in order to gain a broader perspective. In your own words, remind them that there is no quick-fix solution to overturning their immune system. This work could be an opportunity to perceive and appreciate the complexity of their situation. This is also an opportunity to bring their attention to how our own individual stories can shape the group's story and the big assumptions embedded in it.

After each person has finished speaking, invite the group to be silent for a few minutes, then invite feedback. As a way to respect the integrity of the person's sharing and the relationships in the group, you might find it helpful to guide the feedback session with a question such as, "What has touched you in what (name) has shared?"

Step 3: *Closing the conversation* *(20 minutes)*

Once all participants have shared, and there is agreement that the history of the big assumption has been sufficiently explored, close the conversation with a gesture of gratitude for the richness of the discussion. This could be done in the form of spontaneous prayer or a litany of thanksgiving prepared in advance.

Step 4: *Preparing for the next stage* *(5 minutes)*

Invite participants to continue to reflect on the history of their big assumption. Again, remind them not to change their behaviour but continue simply to pay attention to how their big assumption affects their behaviour as a group. Refer them back to the six stages of the follow-up phase and tell them that at the next session, they will begin to design a modest and safe test for their big assumptions. Ask a few people to take responsibility for opening and for closing the next session.

Close with prayer.

Session 3: Stage 4: Design a first test of your big assumption

Step 1: *Welcome, prayer, and check-in* *(15 minutes)*

The people who offered to take responsibility for the opening of this session lead the opening prayer, do check-in, and offer a recap of that session. Participants are invited to share their own experience of that meeting and subsequent reflections.

APPENDIX 4

Step 2: Sharing *(50 minutes)*

Begin with a discussion of how big assumptions are embedded in our competing commitments. To make this clearer, you could use either their own collective four-column exercise or the example in Figure 2 (pages 115–16). Open the space for sharing insights, questions, and concerns. Then, invite the group to design a modest and safe test of their big assumption. This could be done in the form of a brainstorming session in which ideas are recorded on a flipchart. Ask them to name the signs they will look for in testing the validity of their big assumption. You could use the example of the St. Cloud Pastoral Leadership Team. As noted in Figure 2, the team tended to ignore challenging feedback, especially from those who did not agree with the program. Before actually designing a test, the team first discussed what they meant by their big assumption of meeting their target. That clarity enabled them to design their first, modest test, in which they selected five parishioners (whose feedback they realized they had ignored) whom they would invite to a meeting to listen to their experience of the specific changes that were implemented in the weekly Scripture study sessions. While they knew it might be a risk to open the door to a barrage of complaints against all facets of the parish renewal program, they also knew that their big assumption was supporting a top-down approach to ministry that was contrary to their own vision. They felt that this modest test might cast even more doubt on their big assumption. Maybe if they did listen and respond to some of the criticisms, the parish renewal program might not only be on target, but also might become even better and more inclusive in the community.

Step 3: Closing ritual and sending forth prayer *(10 minutes)*

Close the session by first asking people to take responsibility for opening and closing the next session. See Appendix 2 as well as prayer resources for suggestions.

Session 4: Stage 5: Examine the results of your first test

Step 1: Welcome, prayer, and check-in *(15 minutes)*

The people who offered to take responsibility for opening the session lead the prayer, do check-in, and offer a recap of the last session.

Invite participants to share their experience of that session and subsequent reflections.

Step 2: Sharing the results of the first test (50 minutes)

Open the space for sharing and examining the results of their first test. Invite each person to share, guiding them with the following or similar questions:

- What do the results of your test tell you about the validity of your big assumption?
- Is the test more accurate with certain people or in certain circumstances?

As when they shared the history of the big assumption, this is a time for receiving each story with openness and reverence. Provide feedback that will build and support the group in its commitment to change.

Step 3: Preparing for the next stage: Designing the next test (45 minutes)

Invite conversation about the next stage, in which the participants are encouraged to develop further tests. If the group has been meeting regularly every two months, it might prefer to schedule the next session in six months. This would give them time to do further testing. Or they might find the support of facilitated sessions to be very helpful and prefer to meet regularly. Leave this decision to the group; prepare for the next session in a way that supports that choice.

Step 4: Closing ritual and sending forth prayer (10 minutes)

See Appendix 2 and prayer resources for suggestions.

Session 5: Develop, run, and evaluate further tests

As with the individual follow-up phase, participants left the last session with an invitation to design and run further tests. Session 5 and any subsequent sessions would most likely resemble Session 4, in which the group will share the results of their most recent test and, if necessary, design another one. It will be your role to discern with the group when they no longer require the services of an outside facilitator.

APPENDIX 4

Keep in mind that the primary goal of the sessions is to provide a space for working with the group's own resistance to change. Although this is ongoing work, they will probably not require meetings that specifically focus on that goal. You could suggest that they build in time for reflecting on their praxis into their agendas for their regular meetings. For example, after five sessions, the St. Cloud Pastoral Leadership Team allocated 20 minutes in their monthly meetings for a focused conversation on their values and practice. In their calendar for the upcoming year, they also included a retreat day dedicated to reflecting on their vision and commitment to change in their praxis.

Bibliography

Alternative Fuels Research and Education Division of the Railroad Commission of Texas, www.propane.tx.gov/education/objectives.html. Accessed February 19, 2005.

Anderson, E. Byron. *Worship and Christian Identity: Practicing Ourselves*. Collegeville, MN: Liturgical Press, 2003.

Arbuckle, Gerald S.M. *Revisioning the Church: Dissent for Leadership*. Maryknoll, NY: Orbis Books, 1993.

Badcock, Gary D. *Light of Truth & Fire of Love: A Theology of the Holy Spirit*. Grand Rapids, MI: William B. Eerdmans, 1997.

Bassett, Lytta, *Holy Anger: Jacob, Job and Jesus*. Ottawa: Novalis, 2007.

Benedict XVI. 2005. *Deus Caritas Est: Encyclical Letter of the Supreme Pontiff Benedict XVI to the Bishops, Priests and Deacons, Men and Women Religious and All the Faithful on Christian Love*. www.vatican.va/holy_father/benedict_xvi/encyclicals/documents/hf_ben-xvi_enc_20051225_deux-caritas-est_en.html. Accessed 14 March 2006.

Browning, Don S. *A Fundamental Practical Theology: Descriptive and Strategic Proposals*. Minneapolis, MN: Fortress Press, 1996.

Burns, Charlene P. E. "Cognitive Dissonance Theory and the Induced-Compliance Paradigm: Concerns for Teaching Religious Studies." *Teaching Theology and Religion*. Vol. 9:1, 2006. 3-8.

Byrne, Lavinia. *Woman at the Altar: The Ordination of Women in the Roman Catholic Church.* Collegeville, MN: Liturgical Press, 1994.

Canon Law Society of Great Britain and Ireland in association with The Canon Law Society of Australia and New Zealand and The Canadian Canon Law Society, *The Code of Canon Law.* Ottawa: Canadian Conference of Catholic Bishops, 1983.

Catholic News Service, "Pope tells Portuguese Bishops Church Must Involve More Lay People", Nov 12th, 2007. http://www.catholic-news.com/data/briefs/cns/20071112.htm. Accessed November 19, 2007.

Centre for Ministry Formation: *Handbook for Members 2005-2006* (unpublished).

Chadwick, Henry. *The Early Church, Revised Edition.* London: Penguin Books, 1993.

Chapman, J.A. "A Framework for Transformational Change in Organizations" in *Leadership and Organizational Development Journal.* Vol. 23 (1), 2002, 16-25.

Cobb, John B. Jr. *Reclaiming the Church: Where the Mainline Church Went Wrong and What to Do About It.* Louisville, KY: Westminster John Knox Press, 1997.

Daloz Parks, Sharon. *Leadership Can Be Taught: A Bold Approach for a Complex World.* Boston, MA: Harvard Business School Press, 2005.

Doyle, Denis A. *Communion Ecclesiology.* Maryknoll, NY: Orbis Books, 2000.

Dulles, Avery. *Models of Church.* New York: Doubleday, 1987.

Fiorenza, Elisabeth Schüssler. *Discipleship of Equals: A Critical Feminist Ecclesia-logy of Liberation.* New York: Crossroad, 1993.

Fischer, Kathleen. *Transforming Fire: Women Using Anger Creatively.* New York: Paulist Press, 1999.

Flannery, Austin, O.P., general ed. (1996). *The Basic Sixteen Documents Vatican Council II: Constitutions, Decrees and Declarations. A Completely Revised Translation in Inclusive Language.* Northport, NY: Costello Publishing.

Fox, Patricia A. RSM. *God as Communion: John Zizioulas, Elizabeth Johnson and the Retrieval of the Symbol of the Triune God.* Collegeville, MN: The Liturgical Press, 2001.

Freire, Paulo. *Pedagogy of the Oppressed.* New York: Seabury, 1970.

———. *Education for Critical Consciousness.* London: Sheed & Ward, 1973,

Gadamer, Hans-Georg. *Truth and Method.* New York: Seabury Press, 1975.

Gilchrist, Michael. "Liturgy: New improved English translation of the Roman Missal nears completion, in *Catholicinsight.com.* Online Publication Date: Sep 1, 2004, 16:39. http://catholicinsight.com/online/church/liturgy/printer_new_mass.shtml. Accessed November 29, 2007.

Griffiths, Morwenna. *Feminisms and the Self: The Web of Identity.* New York: Routledge, 1995.

Hurtubise, Pierre, O.M.I. *Cum Apostolica Sedes: Centenary of the Pontifical Charter 1889-1989 Saint Paul University.* Ottawa, Ontario: Novalis, 1989.

John Paul II. *Shepherds after my own heart : Post-synodal apostolic exhortation of His Holiness John Paul II on the formation of priests in the circumstances of the present day.* Sherbrooke, QC: Éditions Paulines, 1992.

———. *The New Millenium: Novo Millennio Ineunte. Apostolic Letter of His Holiness Pope John Paul II to the Bishops, Clergy and Lay Faithful at the Close of the Great Jubilee of the Year 2000.* Quebec: Médiaspaul, 2001.

———. "The Laity Have Full Membership In The Church" Audience October 27, 1993 http://www.vatican.va/holy_father/john_paul_ii/audiences/alpha/data/aud19931027en.html. Accessed November 30, 2007.

Johnson, Elizabeth A. *SHE WHO IS: The Mystery of God in Feminist Discourse.* New York: Crossroad Publishing Company, 1992.

Jung, Carl G. *Answer to Job.* New York: Meridian Books, 1960.

Kegan, Robert. *The Evolving Self: Problem and Process in Human Development.* Cambridge: Harvard University Press, 1982.

———. *In Over Our Heads: The Mental Demands of Modern Life.* Cambridge: Harvard University Press, 1994.

Kegan, Robert and Lisa Laskow Lahey. *How the Way We Talk Can Change the Way We Work: Seven Languages of Transformation.* San Francisco: Jossey-Bass, 2001.

———. "The Real Reason People Won't Change" in *Harvard Business Review,* November 2001, Reprint 20110E, 85-93.

Killen, Patricia O'Connell. *Finding Our Voices: Women, Wisdom and Faith.* New York: Crossroad, 1997.

Kinast, Robert. "Co-discipleship: Ministry that is Shared." *Origins* 17. 1987-1988. 585-588.

King, Eugene O.M.I., *Apostolic Visitation to Canadian Seminaries: Report of Saint Paul University Seminary, Ottawa,* September 1993 (unpublished).

LaCugna, Catherine Mowry. *GOD FOR US: The Trinity and Christian Life.* New York: Harper Collins, 1993.

Lee, John D. "Diversity and Community: Babel and Pentecost." *Perspectives: A Journal of Reformed Thought.* Vol. 7 No. 6. June 1992. 12-13.

Lerner, G. *The Feminist Thought of Sarah Grimké.* Oxford, U.K.: Oxford University Press, 1998.

BIBLIOGRAPHY

MacIntyre, Alisdair. *After Virtue: A Study in Moral Theory*, Notre Dame, IN: University of Notre Dame Press, Second Edition, 1984.

Malone, Mary T. *Women and Christianity*, Volumes 1 and 2. Ottawa: Novalis, 2000.

Markey, John P. *Creating Communion: The Theology of the Constitutions of the Church*. Hyde Park, NY: Newcity Press, 2003.

Martin, Joel. "Being as Communion by John D. Zizioulas" in Liturgy, Orthodoxy. *Livingtext.com*. January 14, 2006. http://livingtext.wordpress.com/2006/01/14/being-as-communion-by-john-d-zizioulas/. Accessed December 2, 2007.

Metzger, Bruce M. and Roland E. Murphy, eds. *The New Oxford Annotated Bible*. New York: Oxford University Press, 1991.

Mezirow, Jack and Associates. *Learning as Transformation: Critical Perspectives on a Theory of Progress*. San Francisco: Jossey-Bass, 2000.

National Conference of Catholic Bishops. *The Rites of the Roman Catholic Church Volume II: A Study Edition*. Collegeville, MN: Liturgical Press, 1991.

Nichols, Terence L. *That All May Be One: Hierarchy and Participation in the Church*. Collegeville, MN: Liturgical Press, 1997.

Norris, Richard A. *The Christological Controversy*. Philadelphia: Fortress Press, 1980, 157-159.

O'Collins, Gerald S. J., *The Tripersonal God: Understanding and Interpreting the Trinity*. New York: Paulist Press, 1999.

O'Murchu, Diarmuid. *Catching up with Jesus: A Gospel Story for Our Time*. New York: Crossroad Publishing, 2005.

———. *Evolutionary Faith: Rediscovering God in Our Great Story*. Maryknoll, NY: Orbis Books, 2003.

Papesh, Michael L. "Farewell to 'the Club'" in *America*. Vol. 186, No.16, May 13, 2002. 7-11.

Parent, Rémi. *Church of the Baptized: Overcoming the Tension between Clergy and Laity.* Translated by Stephen W. Arndt. New York: Paulist Press, 1989.

Paver, John. *Theological Reflection and Education for Ministry : The Search for Integration in Theology.* Aldershot, Hampshire, England: Ashgate, 2006.

Pelikan, Jaroslav. *The Emergence of the Catholic Tradition (100-600): The Christian Tradition: A History of the Development of Doctrine, Vol. 1.* Chicago: The University of Chicago Press, 1971.

Perri, William D. *A Radical Challenge for Priesthood Today: From Trial to Transformation.* Mystic, CT: Twenty-Third Publications, 1996.

Ratzinger, Cardinal J. The July 2004 Vatican Statement on Creation and Evolution. *Communion and Stewardship: Human Persons Created in the Image of God.* International Theological Commission. http://www.bringyou.to/apologetics/p80.htm. Accessed August 25, 2006.

Riggs, Marcia Y. "Embracing Race and Ethnicity in Theological Education." *Presentation at the Association of Theological Schools Committee on Race and Ethnicity Conference on "Racial Ethnic Faculty in Predominantly White Institutions" October 5-7, 2001,* http://www.ats.edu/leadership_education/riggs.asp. Accessed August 10, 2007.

Ruether, Rosemary Radford. *Sexism and God-Talk: Toward a Feminist Theology.* Paperback reprint of 1983 edition. Boston, MA: Beacon Press, 1993.

Russell, Letty M. *Human Liberation in a Feminist Perspective.* Philadelphia: Westminster Press, 1974.

———. *Church in the Round: Feminist Interpretation of the Church.* Westminster: John Knox Press, 1993.

BIBLIOGRAPHY

Ste-Marie, Lorraine. "'Immunity-to-Change Language Technology': Educational Tool for Pastoral Leadership Education" in *Teaching Theology and Religion*, ISSN 1368-4868, vol. 11 no. 2, 92–102.

———. *Language and Change: The Immunity-to-Change Language Technology as a Tool for Integrating the Ecclesial Vision of the Centre for Ministry Formation into its Ministry Formation Process.* Doctor of Ministry dissertation, 2005 (unpublished).

Schillebeeckx, Edward. *Ministry: Leadership in the Community of Jesus Christ.* New York: Crossroad, 1981.

———. *The Church with a Human Face: A New and Expanded Theology of Ministry.* New York: Crossroad, 1985.

Sparks, Dennis. "Inner Conflicts, Inner Strengths: Interview with Robert Kegan and Lisa Lahey" in *Journal of Staff Development*, Summer 2002, Volume 23, Number 3.

Stackhouse, Max L. "Ecclesiology and Ethics" in *The Westminster Dictionary of Christian Ethics.* James F. Childress and John Macquarrie, eds. Philadelphia: The Westminster Press, 1986.

Starkloff, Carl F., S.J. *Covenant, Culture and Communion: Church as Model of the Multicultural Common Good in Mission and Interreligious Dialogue:* http://groups.creighton.edu/sjdialogue/documents/articles/church_as_covenant.html. Accessed August 17, 2007.

Taylor, Charles. *Human Agency and Language: Philosophical Papers I.* Cambridge: Cambridge University Press, 1985. Reprinted 1999.

Thompson, William M. *Christ and Consciousness: Exploring Christ's Contribution to Human Consciousness: The Origins and Development of Christian Consciousness.* New York: Paulist Press, 1977.

Tracy, David. *Blessed Rage for Order: The New Pluralism in Theology.* New York: Seabury Press, 1975.

Vanier, Jean. *Community and Growth.* London: Dartman, Longman and Todd. 2nd Revised Edition, 1989.

Wessels, Cletus. *The Holy Web: Church and the New Universe Story.* Maryknoll, NY: Orbis Books, 2000.

Wheatley, Margaret J. *Leadership and the New Science: Discovering Order in a Chaotic World.* San Francisco: Berrett-Koehler Publishers, 1999.

Whitehead, James D. and Evelyn Whitehead. *The Promise of Partnership: A Model for Collaborative Ministry.* New York: Harper Publishers, 1995.

Wilber, Ken. *Integral Spirituality: A Startling New Role for Religion in the Modern and Postmodern World.* Boston: Integral Books, 2006.

Wood, Susan K., ed. *Ordering the Baptismal Priesthood: Theologies of Lay and Ordained Ministry.* Collegeville, MN: Liturgical Press, 2003.

Zizioulas, John D. *Being as Communion: Studies in Personhood and the Church.* Crestwood, NY: St. Vladimir's Press, 1985.

Dictionaries:

Childress, James F. and John Macquarrie, eds. *The Westminster Dictionary of Christian Ethics.* Philadelphia: The Westminster Press, 1986.

Little, William, H.W. Fowler, J. Coulson (Prepared by). *The Shorter Oxford English Dictionary on Historical Principles. Third Edition Revised with Addenda.* Oxford: Clarendon Press, 1956.

Resources for Prayer

Archer-Greene, Rev. Judee, Rev. Richard Vandervaart and Dr. Mary Marrocco (under guidance and leadership). *Liturgies for Christian Unity: The First Hundred Years, 1908–2008*. Ottawa: Novalis, 2008.

Brind, Jan and Tessa Wilkinson. *Creative Ideas for Evening Prayer: For Seasons, Feasts and Special Occasions Throughout the Year*. London: Canterbury Press, 2005.

Brueggemann, Walter. *Awed to Heaven, Rooted in Earth: Prayer of Walter Brueggemann*. Minneapolis, MN: Augsburg Fortress Press, 2002.

Caltagrione, Carmen L. *Together We Pray: Prayers and Services for Gatherings and Groups*. Notre Dame, IN: Ave Maria Press, 2005.

Cocks, Nancy. *Invisible We See You: Tracing Celtic Threads Through Christian Community*. Ottawa: Novalis, 2006.

Cole, Phyllis and Everett Tilson. *Litanies and Other Prayers: For the Revised Common Lectionary, Year A*. Nashville: Abingdon Press, 1992. (Years B and C also available)

Duncan, Geoffrey. *600 Blessings and Prayers: From Around the World*. Mystic, CT: Twenty-Third Publications, 2001.

———. *Harvest for the World: A Worship Anthology on Sharing in the Work of Creation*. Cleveland, OH: Pilgrim Press, 2003.

Hintz, Debra, *Near Us and Within Us: Weekly Prayer Services for Parish Gatherings.* Mystic, CT: Twenty-Third Publications, 2006.

Malone, Mary. *Praying with the Women Mystics.* Ottawa: Novalis, 2006.

O'Donohue, John. *To Bless the Space Between Us.* Audio Book (4 CDs). Louisville, CO: Sounds True, 2008.

O'Murchu, Diarmuid and William Cleary. *Prayers to an Evolutionary God.* Woodstock, VT: Skylight Paths Publishing, 2004.

Pickering, Sue. *Creative Ideas for Quiet Days.* London: Canterbury Press, 2006.

Proctor-Smith, Marjorie. *The Church in Her House: A Feminist Emancipatory Prayer Book for Christian Communities.* Cleveland, OH: Pilgrim Press, 2008.

Ramshaw, Gail, ed. *Intercessions for the Christian People: Cycles A, B, C.* Collegeville, MN: Liturgical Press, 1990.

Roberts, Elizabeth and Elias L. Amidon (eds). *Earth Prayers from Around the World: 365 Prayers, Poems and Invocations for Honoring the Earth.* Toronto: HarperCollins Canada, 1991.

Rowthor, Jefrey W. *The Wisdom of God's Mercy: Litanies to Enlarge Our Prayers.* New York: Church Publishing, 2007.

Skrepichuk, Sylvia and Michel Côté. *We Dare to Say: Prayers for Justice and Peace.* Ottawa: Novalis, 2007.

Tirabassi, Maren C. and Kathy Wonson Eddy. *Gifts of Many Cultures: Worship Resources for the Global Community.* Cleveland, OH: Pilgrim Press, 1995.

Ward, Hannah, Jennifer Wild and Janet Morley. *Celebrating Women.* Harrisburg, PA: Morehouse Publishing, 1995.

Watts, Trisha and Gabrielle Lord. *Sanctuary: Where Heaven Touches Earth.* Northstone, 2005.

Resources for Facilitation

Bens, Ingrid. *Advanced Facilitation Strategies: Tools & Techniques to Master Difficult Situations.* Toronto: John Wiley and Sons, 2005.

Heron, John. *The Complete Facilitator's Handbook.* Philadelphia: Kogan Page, 1999.

Justice, Tom and David W. Jamieson, Ph.D. *The Facilitators' Field: Second Edition.* New York: Amacom, 2006.

Minds at Work™: A Consulting firm that offers training and support for individuals and organizations in working with resistance to change. This firm is run by its founders Robert Kegan and Lisa Lahey and their associates. http://www.mindsatwork.com/

Schwarz, Roger. *The Skilled Facilitator: A Comprehensive Resource for Consultants, Facilitators, Managers, Trainers and Coaches.* San Francisco: Jossey-Bass Publications, 2002.

Smith, Kenwyn K. and David N. Berg, *Paradoxes of Group Life: Understanding Conflict, Paralysis, and Movement in Group Dynamics.* San Francisco: Jossey-Bass, 1997.

Figure 3: Four-column exercise (individual)

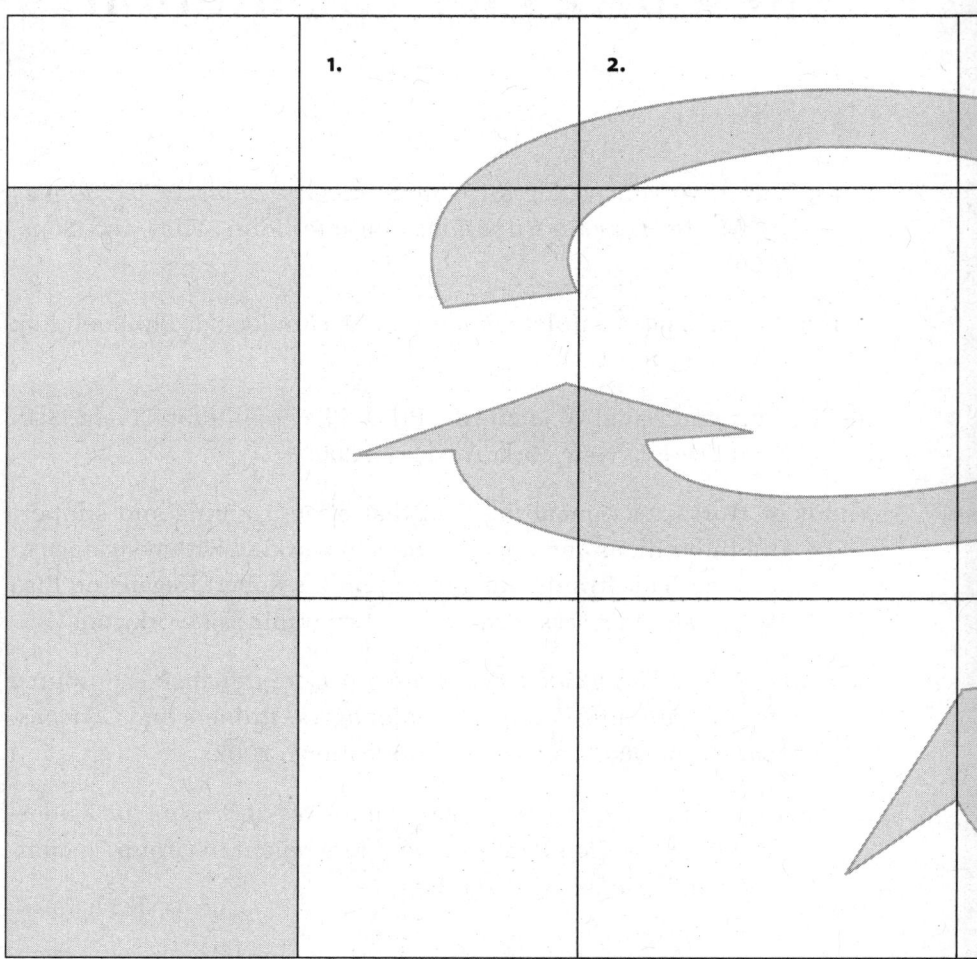

Four-column template © Minds at Work

3.

4.

Figure 4: Four-column exercise (collective)

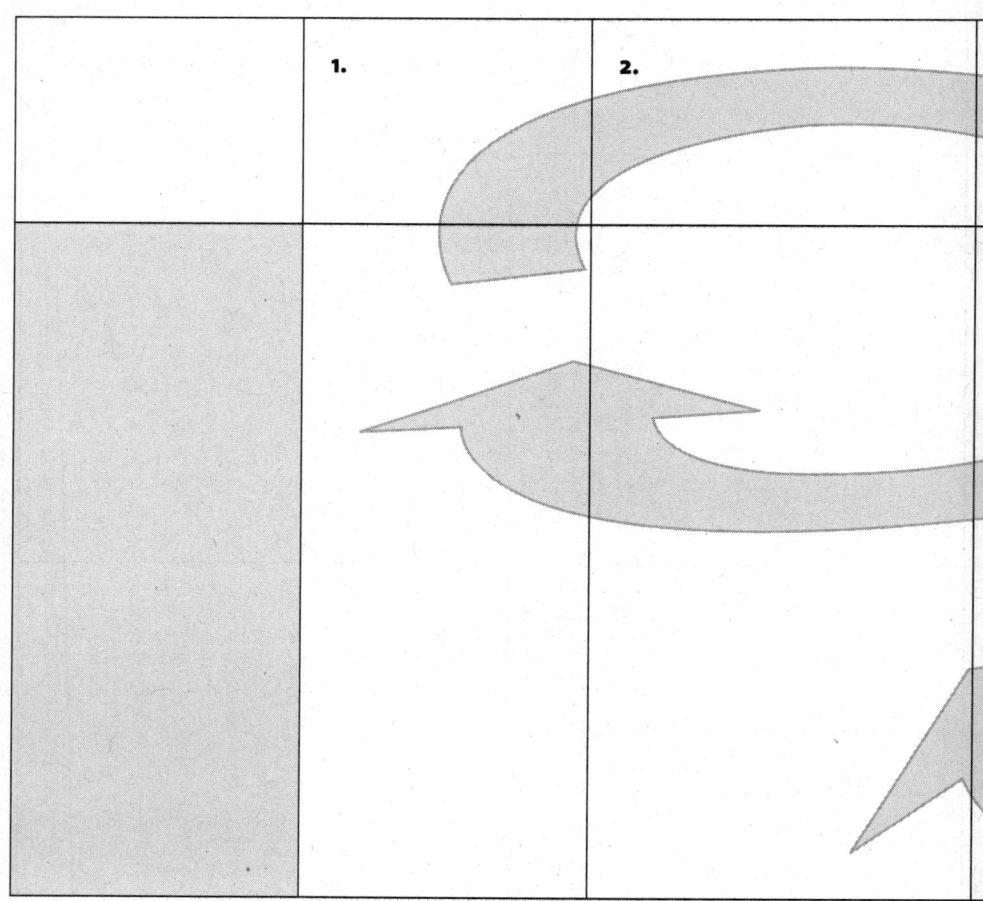

Four-column template © Minds at Work

3.

4.

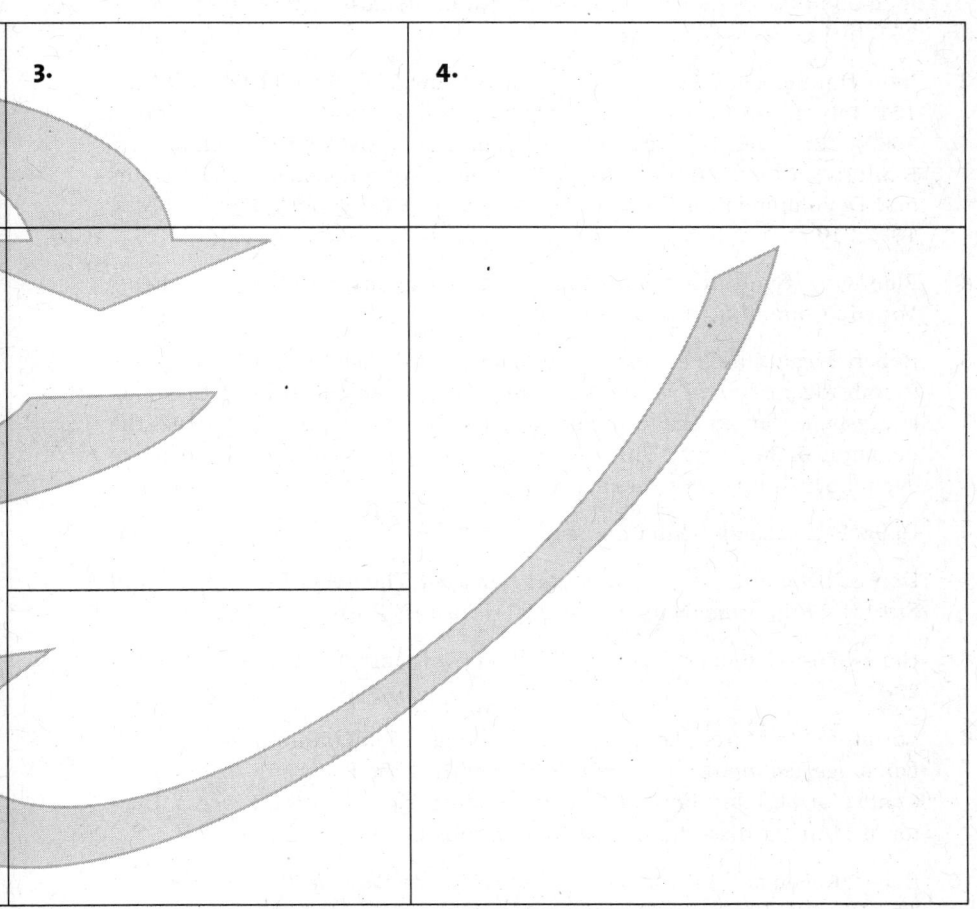

Notes

1. Adapted from Austin Flannery, O.P., General Editor, "Gaudium et Spes," Article 11 in *The Basic Sixteen Documents Vatican Council II: Constitutions, Decrees and Declarations. A Completely Revised Translation in Inclusive Language* (Northport, NY: Costello Publishing, 1996), 173.

2. Cited in Sharon Daloz Parks, *Leadership Can be Taught: A Bold Approach for a Complex World* ((Boston, MA: Harvard Business School Press, 2005)), 257, fn 1.

3. John Dunne, *The Way of All the Earth* (New York: Paulist Press, 1972), 151, relying on Carl Jung, *Answer to Job* (New York: Meridian Books, 1960), 185, cited in Thompson, William M., *Christ and Consciousness: Exploring Christ's Contribution to Human Consciousness: The Origins and Development of Christian Consciousness* (New York: Paulist Press, 1977), 10.

4. Flannery, "Gaudium et Spes," Article 4 in *The Basic Sixteen Documents Vatican Council II,* 165.

5. Robert Kegan, *In Over Our Heads: The Mental Demands of Modern Life* (Cambridge: Harvard University Press, 1994). As the title of the book suggests, Kegan argues throughout that we are not equipped to meet the demands of modernity. This loss of grounding is exacerbated as we move even more deeply into postmodernity.

6. Daloz Parks, *Leadership Can Be Taught*, 2.

7. Don S. Browning, *A Fundamental Practical Theology: Descriptive and Strategic Proposals* (Minneapolis, MN: Fortress Press, 1996), 62.

8. Hans-Georg Gadamer, *Truth and Method* (New York: Seabury Press, 1975), 238.

9. Lorraine Ste-Marie, *Language and Change: The Immunity-to-Change Language Technology as a Tool for Integrating the Ecclesial Vision of the Centre for Ministry Formation into its Ministry Formation Process*. Doctor of Ministry dissertation, 2005. (unpublished).

10. Robert Kegan and Lisa Laskow Lahey, *How the Way We Talk Can Change The Way We Work: Seven Languages of Transformation* (San Francisco: Jossey-Bass, 2001).

11. Daloz Parks, *Leadership Can Be Taught*, 9.

12. Elizabeth A. Johnson, *She Who Is: The Mystery of God in Feminist Discourse* (New York: Crossroad, 1992), 223.

13. Catherine Mowry LaCugna, *God for Us: The Trinity and Christian Life* (New York: Harper Collins, 1993), 343.

Notes

14 Paulo Freire, *Pedagogy of the Oppressed* (New York: Seabury, 1970), 28.

15 Jean Vanier, *Community and Growth* (London: Dartman, Longman and Todd, 1989), 105.

16 Browning, *A Fundamental Practical Theology*, 44–45, in referring to the insights of George Lindbeck: *The Nature of Doctrine: Religion and Theology in a Postliberal Age* (Philadelphia, PA: Westminster Press, 1984).

17 Parent, *Church of the Baptized*, 157. Italics added for emphasis.

18 Daloz Parks, *Leadership Can Be Taught*, 6.

19 Jung, *Answer to Job*, 185 cited in Thompson, *Christ and Consciousness*, 10.

20 Kegan and Lahey, *How the Way We Talk Can Change the Way We Work*.

21 *The Shorter Oxford English Dictionary on Historical Principles. Third Edition Revised with Addenda*. Prepared by William Little, H.W. Fowler, J. Coulson (Oxford: Clarendon Press, 1956), "word".

22 Kegan and Lahey, *How the Way We Talk Can Change the Way We Work*, 3.

23 Kegan, *In Over Our Heads*, 29.

24 Kegan, *In Over Our Heads*, 33. While Kegan uses the term "higher" knowing, he qualifies "higher" as being more complex and inclusive.

25 Thompson, *Christ and Consciousness*, 6.

26 For a comprehensive study of the church's historical development including its five councils, see Jaroslav Pelikan, *The Emergence of the Catholic Tradition (100–600): The Christian Tradition: A History of the Development of Doctrine*, vol. 1 (Chicago: The University of Chicago Press, 1971). This volume is part of larger work entitled *The Christian Tradition: A History of the Development of Doctrine, Volumes 1 to 5* (Chicago: University of Chicago Press, 1971–1989).

27 Flannery, "Decree on Ecumenism," Article 6 in *Sixteen Documents Vatican Council II*, 507.

28 Letty M. Russell, *Church in the Round: Feminist Interpretation of the Church* (Westminster: John Knox Press, 1993), 30.

29 Kathleen Fischer, *Transforming Fire: Women Using Anger Creatively* (New York: Paulist Press, 1999), 9.

30 Lytta Bassett, *Holy Anger: Jacob, Job and Jesus* (Ottawa: Novalis, 2007).

31 Patricia O'Connell Killen, *Finding Our Voices: Women, Wisdom and Faith* (New York: Crossroad, 1997), 24.

32 Killen, *Finding Our Voices*, 21.

33 Paulo Freire, *Education for Critical Consciousness* (London: Sheed & Ward, 1973), 4. Italics in original text.

34 Killen, *Finding Our Voices*, 6.

35 *The Code of Canon Law* (Ottawa: Concacan, 1983). Canon 277, par. 1. One could favourably argue that the permanent diaconate opens up ministry to married males. However, if he is not married prior to ordination, he must publicly undertake the vow to celibacy (Canon 1037). Also, if the permanent deacon's wife dies before him, he cannot remarry without dispensation from Rome. The Congregation for Divine Worship and Discipline of the Sacraments does recommend that dispensation be granted to a widowed deacon, permitting him to remarry, if: he has the care of minor children; the care of elderly or infirm parents; or the serious needs of the particular church for which the deacon is exceptionally useful.

36 Caroline Hennessey, *I. B.I.T.C.H., Have Had It* (Canada: Lancer Books, 1970).

37 John Paver, *Theological Reflection and Education for Ministry: The Search for Integration in Theology* (Aldershot, Hampshire, England: Ashgate, 2006), 67, in reference to Sally McFague Teselle, *Speaking in Parables: A Study in Metaphor and Theology* (Philadelphia: Fortress Press, 1975), 157–61.

38 Jung, *Answer to Job*, 185.

39 Eugene King, O.M.I., *Apostolic Visitation to Canadian Seminaries: Report of Saint Paul University Seminary, Ottawa*. September 1993 (unpublished), 5–6. The "Historical Notes" in this report provide the basis for the first three ages in ministry formation in Saint Paul Seminary.

40 Pierre Hurtubise, o.m.i., *Cum Apostolica Sedes: Centenary of the Pontifical Charter 1889–1989, Saint Paul University* (Ottawa, 1989), 79. This publication has been invaluable for this historical review.

41 King, *Apostolic Visitation to Canadian Seminaries*, 5.

42 King, *Apostolic Visitation to Canadian Seminaries*, 5–6.

43 All Roman Catholic seminaries must follow the canonical norms.

44 Louise Auclair stands as a beacon in the struggle for living the vision of moving toward a more inclusive church. Louise died of leukemia in September 2001. This book is dedicated to her.

45 John Paul II *Shepherds After My Own Heart: Post-Synodal Apostolic Exhortation of His Holiness John Paul II on the Formation of Priests in the Circumstances of the Present Day* (Sherbrooke, QC: Éditions Paulines, 1992).

Notes

46 The Centre for Ministry Formation: *Handbook for Members, 2005–2006* (unpublished). This same movement has been articulated in its original vision statement dating back to 1996.

47 Charles Taylor, *Human Agency and Language: Philosophical Papers I* (Cambridge: Cambridge University Press, 1985), 270.

48 John B. Cobb Jr., *Reclaiming the Church: Where the Mainline Church Went Wrong and What to Do About It* (Louisville, KY: Westminster John Knox Press, 1997), 20.

49 For example, the Sisters of Presentation of the Blessed Virgin Mary (PBVM), the Congregation of Notre Dame (CND), and the Sisters of the Holy Name of Jesus and Mary (SNJM).

50 Diarmuid O'Murchu, *Evolutionary Faith: Rediscovering God in Our Great Story* (Maryknoll, NY: Orbis Books, 2003).

51 Cletus Wessels, *The Holy Web: Church and the New Universe Story* (Maryknoll, NY: Orbis Books, 2000).

52 Margaret J. Wheatley, *Leadership and the New Science: Discovering Order in a Chaotic World* (San Francisco: Berrett-Koehler Publishers, 1999).

53 O'Murchu, *Evolutionary Faith*, 10.

54 Ratzinger, Cardinal J. 2004. *The July 2004 Vatican Statement on Creation and Evolution. Communion and Stewardship: Human Persons Created in the Image of God.* International Theological Commission. http://www.bringyou.to/apologetics/p80.htm, para. 69 (accessed 25 August 2006)

55 O'Murchu, *Evolutionary Faith*, 59.

56 Wessels, *Holy Web*, 113.

57 Robert Kinast, "Co-discipleship: Ministry That Is Shared." *Origins* 17. 1987–1988. 585–88.

58 Peter Senge, C. Otto Scharmer, Joseph Jaworski and Betty Sue Flowers, *Presence: An Exploration of Profound Change in People, Organizations and Society* (New York: Doubleday, 2004).

59 Russell, *Church in the Round*, 23.

60 Lavinia Byrne, *Woman at the Altar: The Ordination of Women in the Roman Catholic Church* (Collegeville, MN: Liturgical Press, 1994), 57.

61 Patricia A. Fox, *God as Communion: John Zizioulas, Elizabeth Johnson and the Retrieval of the Symbol of the Triune God* (Collegeville, MN: The Liturgical Press, 2001), 18.

62 Johnson, *She Who Is*, 40.

63 Michael Gilchrist, "Liturgy: New Improved English Translation of the Roman Missal Nears Completion, in *Catholicinsight.com*. Online Publication Date: Sep 1, 2004, 16:39. http://catholicinsight.com/online/church/liturgy/printer_new_mass.shtml (accessed November 29, 2007)

64 Johnson, *She Who Is*, 240.

65 Wessels, *Holy Web*, 81.

66 Alternative Fuels Research and Education Division of the Railroad Commission of Texas, www.propane.tx.gov/education/objectives.html (accessed February 19, 2005)

67 Benedict XVI. 2005. *Deus Caritas Est: Encyclical Letter of the Supreme Pontiff Benedict XVI to the Bishops, Priests and Deacons, Men and Women Religious and All the Faithful on Christian Love*, para. 16. www.vatican.va/holy_father/benedict_xvi/encyclicals/documents/hf_ben-xvi_enc_20051225_deux-caritas-est_en.html (accessed 14 March 2006)

68 O'Murchu, *Evolutionary Faith*, 67.

69 Killen, *Finding Our Voices*, 76.

70 Ken Wilber, *Integral Spirituality: A Startling New Role for Religion in the Modern and Postmodern World* (Boston: Integral Books, 2006), 142.

71 Ken Wilber, *Sex, Ecology, Spirituality: The Spirit of Evolution* (Boston: Shambhala, 1995), viii, as cited in Wessels, *Holy Web*, 57.

72 Wilber, *Integral Spirituality*, 148.

73 O'Murchu, *Evolutionary Faith*, 22.

74 O'Murchu, *Evolutionary Faith*, 177.

75 O'Murchu, *Evolutionary Faith*, 120.

76 O'Murchu, *Evolutionary Faith*, 13.

77 Charles Taylor, "Hegel's Philosophy of Mind" in *Human Agency and Language: Philosophical Papers* 1, 77–96.

78 Marcia Y. Riggs, "Embracing Race and Ethnicity in Theological Education." Presentation at the Association of Theological Schools Committee on Race and Ethnicity Conference on "Racial Ethnic Faculty in Predominantly White Institutions" October 5–7, 2001, www.ats.edu/leadership_education/riggs.asp (accessed August 10, 2007)

79 Cobb, *Reclaiming the Church*, 11.

80 Killen, *Finding Our Voices*, 60.

Notes

81 Gerda Lerner, *The Feminist Thought of Sarah Grimké* (Oxford, UK: Oxford University Press, 1998).

82 Mary T. Malone, *Women and Christianity*, Volumes 1 and 2 (Ottawa: Novalis, 2000 and 2002).

83 Morwenna Griffiths, *Feminisms and the Self: The Web of Identity* (New York: Routledge, 1995), 6.

84 Griffiths, *Feminisms and the Self*, 67.

85 Friends of Sabeel North America: Voice of the Palestinian Christians. http://www.fosna.org/resources/list_of_films.html (accessed July 28, 2007)

86 Browning, *Fundamental Practical Theology*, 6.

87 LaCugna, *God for Us*, 228.

88 Wheatley, *Leadership and the New Science*, 76.

89 Wheatley, *Leadership and the New Science*, 83.

90 Wheatley *Leadership and the New Science*, 85.

91 Wheatley, *Leadership and the New Science*, 85.

92 Wheatley *Leadership and the New Science*, 118.

93 Wheatley, *Leadership and the New Science*, 85.

94 Wheatley, *Leadership and the New Science*, 82.

95 Wheatley, *Leadership and the New Science*, 82.

96 Fischer, *Transforming Fire*, 9.

97 Fischer, *Transforming Fire*, 10.

98 Johnson, *She Who Is*, 223.

99 John P. Markey, *Creating Communion: The Theology of the Constitutions of the Church* (Hyde Park, NY: Newcity Press, 2003), 101.

100 LaCugna, *God for Us*, 1.

101 LaCugna, *God for Us*, 246.

102 LaCugna, *God for Us*, 17.

103 Fox, *God as Communion*, 12.

104 Fox, *God as Communion*, 113.

105 Pelikan, *The Emergence of the Catholic Tradition (100–600)*, 221.

106 Cobb, *Reclaiming the Church*, 17.

107 This is found in the opening prayer in *Mass 367-A; Lectionary ferial*. The memorial of Saint Andrew Dung-Lac and Companions, martyrs.

108 Fox, *God as Communion*, 18.

109 LaCugna, *God for Us*, 1.

110 See John Zizioulas, *Being as Communion: Studies in Personhood and the Church* (Crestwood, NY: St. Vladimir's Press, 1985).

111 Cappadocia, which lies in the heart of Asia Minor (now Turkey), became an important centre of Christian theology in the fourth century. Four leading figures greatly influenced the christological debates leading to the Chalcedonian text: Basil the Great, bishop of Caesarea in Cappadocia (330–379); Gregory of Nazianzus, bishop of Sassima in Cappadocia as well as Archbishop of Constantinople (330–390), Gregory, the younger brother of Basil, bishop of Nyssa (335–94); and, Amphilochius, bishop of Iconium (339–403).

112 Richard A. Norris, *The Christological Controversy* (Philadelphia: Fortress Press, 1980), 155–59.

113 The Council of Chalcedon, AD 451, acknowledged in Christ the hypostatic union of two natures without confusion, without change, without division, and without separation. *Hypostasis* is understood as Communion, *prosopon* as person, and *ousia* as substance. While the text of the Chalcedonian formula continues to be fundamental to the Christological development throughout the Latin West, and much of the East, there continues to be much controversy as to the interpretation of that formula, particularly with respect to the Greek terms of *hypostasis*, *ousia*, and *prosopon*. Jaroslav Pelikan, *The Emergence of the Catholic Tradition (100–600)*, 262–64.

114 Zizioulas, *Being as Communion*, 41.

115 Joel Martin, "Being As Communion by John D. Zizioulas" in *Liturgy, Orthodoxy*. Livingtext.com. January 14, 2006. http://livingtext.wordpress.com/2006/01/14/being-as-communion-by-john-d-zizioulas/ (accessed December 2, 2007)

116 The *filioque* doctrine deals with the relation between the Son and the Holy Spirit. The source of the *filioque* is found in the Latin form of the Creed in AD 381, which states that the Spirit proceeds from both the Father *and* the Son. This has never been accepted in the Christian East, which maintains that Spirit proceeds from the Father, thereby maintaining the monarchic identity of the Father who begets both Son and Spirit. See contribution of Dietrich Ritschl, "The History of the Filioque Controversy" and Michael Fahey, "Son and Spirit: Divergent Theologies between Constantinople and the West," in Hans Küng and Jürgen Moltmann, eds., *Conflicts About*

the *Holy Spirit* (New York: Seabury Press, 1979). This reference is cited from Gary D. Badcock, *Light of Truth & Fire of Love: A Theology of the Holy Spirit* (Grand Rapids, MI: William B. Eerdmans, 1997), 75.

117 Badcock, *Light of Truth*, 76.

118 Badcock, *Light of Truth*, 84.

119 LaCugna, *God for Us*, 98.

120 Badcock, *Light of Truth*, 79.

121 Johnson, *She Who Is*, 220.

122 Johnson, *She Who Is*, 220.

123 Johnson, *She Who Is*, 220.

124 LaCugna, *God for Us*, 270.

125 LaCugna, *God for Us*, 271.

126 Badcock, *Light of Truth*, 200, in reference to Jürgen Moltmann, *The Trinity and the Kingdom of God*, Margaret Kohl, trans. (London: SCM Press, 1981), 150, 174–76. Italics added.

127 Johnson, *She Who Is*, 220.

128 LaCugna, *God for Us*, 296.

129 LaCugna, *God for Us*, 296.

130 LaCugna, *God for Us*, 296.

131 LaCugna, *God for Us*, 296.

132 E. Byron Anderson: *Worship and Christian Identity: Practicing Ourselves* (Collegeville, MN: Liturgical Press, 2003), 197.

133 LaCugna, *God for Us*, 296. LaCugna favours the use of *divinizing*, or as the Eastern tradition names it, "theosis." As we seek to transcend the divide between the sacred and secular, we can see that divinizing is about becoming more human; theosis is about emptying ourselves (kenosis) for the sake of the other.

134 Johnson, *She Who Is*, 134. For Johnson, God's energizing Spirit dwells in all things (Wisdom 12:1) and encompasses the world as a great matrix (Acts 17:28).

135 O'Murchu, *Evolutionary Faith*, 200.

136 For example, Gerald O'Collins, S.J., *The Tripersonal God: Understanding and Interpreting the Trinity* (New York: Paulist Press, 1999), 177–82; John Zizioulas, "Pneumatological Dimension of the Church," *Communion*

International Catholic Review 1 (1974):151; Zizioulas, "Ordination and Communion," Study Encounter 6 (1970):191. Also, see Fox, God as Communion, 76, for her critique of Zizioulas.

137 Johnson, She Who Is, 232.

138 Johnson, She Who Is, 231.

139 Fox, God as Communion, 132.

140 Fox, God as Communion, 133.

141 Fox, God as Communion, 133.

142 Wessels, Holy Web, 30.

143 Johnson, She Who Is, 233.

144 Carl F. Starkloff, S.J., Covenant, Culture and Communion: Church as Model of The Multicultural Common Good in Mission and Interreligious Dialogue: http://groups.creighton.edu/sjdialogue/documents/articles/church_as_covenant.html (accessed August 17, 2007)

145 Starkloff, Covenant, Culture and Communion.

146 Wessels, Holy Web, 87.

147 LaCugna, God for Us, n.22.

148 Doyle, Communion Ecclesiology, 139, quoting Elizabeth Johnson, Friends of God and Prophets: A Feminist Theological Reading of the Communion of Saints (Ottawa: Novalis, 1998), 240.

149 Zizioulas, Being as Communion, 216. In keeping with the vision of moving toward a more inclusive Church, I have expanded on Zizioulas's contention that ordained ministers include publicly mandated pastoral leaders. Also, see Richard R. Gaillardetz, "Ecclesiological Foundations of Ministry in an Ordered Communion" in Susan K. Wood, ed., Ordering the Baptismal Priesthood: Theologies of Lay and Ordained Ministry (Collegeville, MN: Liturgical Press, 2003).

150 For example, in Diarmuid O'Murchu, Catching up with Jesus: A Gospel Story for Our Time (New York: Crossroad Publishing, 2005), the person of Jesus Christ is referred to as the "relational matrix."

151 Jurgen Moltmann, Theologie des Hoffnung. Untersuchungen zur Begründungund zu den Konsequenzen einer christlichen Eschatologie, Beiträge zur evangelischen Theologie, no. 38 (Munich, Chrs. Kaiser Verlag, 1966), 266, cited in Parent, Church of the Baptized, 190.

152 Elisabeth Schüssler Fiorenza, Discipleship of Equals: A Critical Feminist Ecclesia-logy of Liberation (New York: Crossroad, 1993), 30.

Notes

153 Henry Chadwick, *The Early Church, Revised Edition* (London: Penguin, 1993).

154 Max L. Stackhouse, "Ecclesiology and Ethics," in *The Westminster Dictionary of Christian Ethics*, ed. James F. Childress and John Macquarrie (Philadelphia: The Westminster Press, 1986).

155 Letty Russell, *Human Liberation in a Feminist Perspective* (Philadelphia: Westminster Press, 1974), 79.

156 Alisdair MacIntyre, *After Virtue: A Study in Moral Theory, Second Edition* (Notre Dame, IN: University of Notre Dame Press, 1984), 221–23.

157 Russell, *Human Liberation*, 79.

158 Flannery, "Pastoral Constitution on the Church in the Modern World: Gaudium et Spes," article 11 in *Sixteen Documents Vatican II*, 173.

159 Flannery, "Gaudium et Spes," articles 1 and 2 in *Sixteen Documents Vatican Council II*, 163–64.

160 LaCugna, *God for Us*, 322.

161 Flannery, "Lumen Gentium," article 8 in *Sixteen Documents Vatican Council II*, 9.

162 As noted in Flannery, "Lumen Gentium," article 8, *Sixteen Documents Vatican Council II*, 9.

163 Avery Dulles, *Models of Church: Expanded Edition* (New York: Doubleday, 1987), 201.

164 Dulles, *Models of Church*, 202.

165 Flannery, "Lumen Gentium," article 4, in *Sixteen Documents Vatican Council II*, 17.

166 Flannery, "Decree on Ecumenism," article 6 in *Sixteen Documents Vatican Council II*, 507.

167 Parent, *Church of the Baptized*, 157.

168 Flannery, "Lumen Gentium," article 18, in *Sixteen Documents Vatican Council II*, 25.

169 Doyle, *Communion Ecclesiology*, 18. In this multidimensional ecclesial vision, the contrast between the mystical and socio-historical is one of the biggest points of tension in Catholic ecclesiology today. Those who explicitly stress the Mystical Body of Christ image over the People of God image include Henri de Lubac, Hans Urs von Balthasar, Joseph Ratzinger, and John Paul II. While the parameters and focus of this book do not allow for exploring the full range of communion ecclesiologies, we

cannot ignore or dismiss this significant contrast or reduce communion ecclesiology to simply the community of disciples model of church. The community of disciples model which I explore is intended to hold the various dimensions of church as communion in tension.

170 Doyle, *Communion Ecclesiology*, 13.

171 Dulles, *Models of Church*, 218.

172 Centre for Ministry Formation: "Mission Statement" in *Handbook for Members*.

173 Michael Papesh, "Farewell to 'the Club,'" in *America*, Vol. 186, No.16, May 13, 2002, 7–11.

174 Papesh, "Farewell to 'the Club,'" 11.

175 Gerald Arbuckle, S.M. *Revisioning the Church: Dissent for Leadership* (Maryknoll, NY: Orbis Books, 1993), 3.

176 Edward Schillebeeckx, *The Church with a Human Face: A New and Expanded Theology of Ministry* (New York: Crossroad, 1985), 83.

177 Patrick Granfield, *The Limits of the Papacy* (New York: Crossroad, 1987), 58, in Wessels, *Holy Web*, 150.

178 Schillebeeckx, *The Church with a Human Face*, 117.

179 Edward Schillebeeckx, *Ministry: Leadership in the Community of Jesus Christ* (New York: Crossroad, 1981), 13.

180 Schillebeeckx, *Ministry*, 17.

181 Schillebeeckx, *Ministry*, 36–37.

182 Schillebeeckx, *The Church with a Human Face*, 116.

183 Schillebeeckx, *Ministry*, 13.

184 Schillebeeckx, *The Church with a Human Face*, 116.

185 Schillebeeckx, *Ministry*, 18.

186 Schillebeeckx, *Ministry*, 42.

187 National Conference of Catholic Bishops, *The Rites of the Roman Catholic Church Volume II: A study edition* (Collegeville, MN: Liturgical Press, 1991).

188 See Papesh, "Farewell to 'the Club,'" 7–11. In this article, Papesh tells the story of a bishop's offering these words of greeting during the sign of peace at the ordination ceremony.

189 Schillebeeckx, *Ministry*, 19.

NOTES

190 Schillebeeckx, *The Church with a Human Face*, 2.

191 John Paul II, "The Laity Have Full Membership In the Church" Audience October 27, 1993 http://www.vatican.va/holy_father/john_paul_ii/audiences/alpha/data/aud19931027en.html (accessed Nov 30, 2007)

192 Parent, *Church of the Baptized*, 83.

193 Parent, *Church of the Baptized*, 27–28.

194 Parent, *Church of the Baptized*, 87.

195 John Paul II, *The New Millenium: Novo Millennio Ineunte. Apostolic Letter of His Holiness Pope John Paul II to the Bishops, Clergy and Lay Faithful at the Close of the Great Jubilee of the Year 2000* (Quebec: Médiaspaul, 2001), para. 48.

196 Parent, *Church of the Baptized*, 30–31.

197 Wessels, *Holy Web*, 113.

198 Wessels, *Holy Web*, 162.

199 Parent, *Church of the Baptized*, 133 (emphasis original).

200 Bruce M. Metzger, and Roland E. Murphy, eds. *The New Oxford Annotated Bible* (New York: Oxford University Press, 1991), 14 OT.

201 Fiorenza, *Discipleship of Equals*, 186.

202 Fiorenza, *Discipleship of Equals*, 12.

203 Fiorenza, *Discipleship of Equals*, 32.

204 Fiorenza, *Discipleship of Equals*, 15.

205 Fiorenza, *Discipleship of Equals*, 10.

206 Fiorenza, *Discipleship of Equals*, 186.

207 Fiorenza, *Discipleship of Equals*, 185.

208 Fiorenza, *Discipleship of Equals*, 178.

209 Fiorenza, *Discipleship of Equals*, 273.

210 Wessels, *Holy Web*, 57.

211 Wessels, *Holy Web*, 131.

212 Terence L. Nichols, *That All May Be One: Hierarchy and Participation in the Church* (Collegeville, MN: Liturgical Press, 1997), 15.

213 Wessels, *Holy Web*, 58.

214 Nichols, *That All May Be One*, 16.

215 Nichols, *That All May Be One*, 17.

216 Wessels, *Holy Web*, 61.

217 Wessels, *Holy Web*, 163.

218 Wessels, *Holy Web*, 168.

219 Wessels, *Holy Web*, 168.

220 Parent, *Church of the Baptized*, 191.

221 Wessels, *Holy Web*, 171. Also, see Wood, *Ordering the Baptismal Priesthood*, for discussions on other possibilities.

222 Wessels, *Holy Web*, 160.

223 Papesh, "Farewell to 'the Club,'" 11.

224 Wessels, *Holy Web*, 163.

225 Wessels, *Holy Web*, 163.

226 An earlier version of this chapter appeared in an article published in *Teaching Theology and Religion*, published by Blackwell. Lorraine Ste-Marie, "'Immunity-to-Change Language Technology': Educational Tool for Pastoral Leadership Education" in *Teaching Theology and Religion*, ISSN 1368-4868, vol. 11 no. 2, 92–102.

227 Kegan and Lahey, *How the Way We Talk Can Change the Way We Work*, 1.

228 Taylor, *Human Agency and Language*, 270.

229 Mezirow, "Learning to Think Like An Adult" in Mezirow and Associates, *Learning as Transformation: Critical Perspectives on a Theory of Progress* (San Francisco: Jossey-Bass, 2000), 18.

230 See Catholic News Service, "Pope tells Portuguese Bishops Church Must Involve More Lay People", Nov 12, 2007, in which this simultaneous commitment is echoed. http://www.catholicnews.com/data/briefs/cns/20071112.htm (accessed November 19, 2007)

231 See Kegan, *Evolving Self*, 1982, and Kegan, *In Over Our Heads*, 1994.

232 Kegan, *In Over Our Heads*, 32.

233 Kegan and Lahey, *How the Way We Talk Can Change the Way We Work*, 5.

234 Johnson, *She Who Is*, 40.

235 Kegan and Lahey, *How the Way We Talk Can Change the Way We Work*, 7. (Italics in original text.)

236 Kegan and Lahey, *How the Way We Talk Can Change the Way We Work*, 7.

Notes

237 Dennis Sparks, "Inner Conflicts, Inner Strengths: Interview with Robert Kegan and Lisa Lahey," in *Journal of Staff Development*, Summer 2002, Volume 23, Number 3, 69.

238 Sparks, "Inner Conflicts, Inner Strengths," 67 and 69.

239 Parent, *Church of the Baptized*, 133. (Emphasis original).

240 Kegan and Lahey, *How the Way We Talk Can Change the Way We Work*, 64.

241 Papesh, "Farewell to 'the Club,'" 7–11.

242 Kegan and Lahey, *How the Way We Talk Can Change the Way We Work*, 13.

243 Kegan and Lahey, *How the Way We Talk Can Change the Way We Work*, 31.

244 Kegan and Lahey, *How the Way We Talk Can Change the Way We Work*, 28.

245 Kegan and Lahey, *How the Way We Talk Can Change the Way We Work*, 33.

246 Kegan and Lahey, *How the Way We Talk Can Change the Way We Work*, 43.

247 Kegan and Lahey, *How the Way We Talk Can Change the Way We Work*, 37–38.

248 Papesh, "Farewell to 'the Club,'" 7–11.

249 Kegan and Lahey, *How the Way We Talk Can Change the Way We Work*, 47.

250 Kegan and Lahey, *How the Way We Talk Can Change the Way We Work*, 47.

251 Charlene P.E. Burns, "Cognitive Dissonance Theory and the Induced-Compliance Paradigm: Concerns for Teaching Religious Studies." *Teaching Theology and Religion* 2006, Vol. 9:1, 3.

252 Kegan and Lahey, *How the Way We Talk Can Change the Way We Work*, 49.

253 Kegan and Lahey, *How the Way We Talk Can Change the Way We Work*, 67.

254 Kegan, *In Over Our Heads*, 207.

255 Robert Kegan and Lisa Laskow Lahey, "The Real Reason People Won't Change," *Harvard Business Review* November 2001, Reprint 20110E, 85–93, 90.

256 Kegan and Lahey, *How the Way We Talk Can Change the Way We Work*, 74.

257 Kegan and Lahey, *How the Way We Talk Can Change the Way We Work*, 80.

258 Kegan and Lahey, *How the Way We Talk Can Change the Way We Work*, 74.

259 Kegan and Lahey, *How the Way We Talk Can Change the Way We Work*, 1.

260 Wessels, *Holy Web*, 163.

261 Parent, *Church of the Baptized*, 191.

262 Parent, *Church of the Baptized*, 192.

263 LaCugna, *God for Us*, 296.

264 E. Byron Anderson: *Worship and Christian Identity: Practicing Ourselves* (Collegeville, MN: Liturgical Press, 2003), 197.

265 Flannery, "Pastoral Constitution on the Church in the Modern World: Gaudium et Spes," article 11 in *Sixteen Documents Vatican Council II*, 173.

266 *Catholic Encyclopedia*: Liturgy. www.newadvent.org/cathen/09306a.htm (accessed December 12, 2007)

267 The New Testament Greek Lexicon: http://www.studylight.org/lex/grk/view.cgi?number=3009 (accessed December 12, 2007)

268 Flannery, "The Constitution on the Sacred Liturgy," article 14 in *Sixteen Documents Vatican Council II*, 124.

269 Jung, *Answer to Job*, 185.

270 Thompson, *Christ and Consciousness*, 8.

271 Parent, *Church of the Baptized*, 51.

272 Fiorenza, *Discipleship of Equals*, 1. This is taken from a song from a women's movement in Germany (author unknown).

273 O'Murchu, *Evolutionary Faith*, 22.

274 O'Murchu, *Evolutionary Faith*, 20.

275 I am indebted to Colleen Mahoney, ssa, for introducing me to this practice.